Dr Pixie's
First Foods

igloobooks

To Mini, my very own super mum

Published in 2015
by Igloo Books Ltd
Cottage Farm
Sywell
NN6 0BJ
www.igloobooks.com

Text © 2015 Pixie McKenna
Design and layout © 2015 Igloo Books Ltd
Food photography and recipe development
© Stockfood, The Food Media Agency

LEO002 1115
2 4 6 8 10 9 7 5 3 1
ISBN 978-1-78440-831-2

Cover image © Alexandra Grablewski / Getty Images
Image of Pixie McKenna © Louise Young

Cover designed by Nicholas Gage
Interiors designed by Charles Wood-Penn
Edited by Vicky Taylor

Printed and manufactured in China

"The most important thing is that when the time comes to engage with this next baby phase you embrace it."

Contents

 When you see this symbol, it means the recipe is suitable for home freezing.

Foreword

If babies were a commodity they would come with reams of instructions! Instead your baby lands on your lap and you have to feel your way from zero to one. That first year is like competing in the Olympic hurdles. There are lots of jumps – sometimes you quickly get past them, other times you fall at the first fence. You watch your peers do it seemingly so easily and the world watches you taking jump after jump, or so it feels. Some of the hurdles that appear insurmountable at the start end up being straightforward. Some of the simple jumps catch you by surprise. No two performances are the same, just like no two babies are the same. Look inside yourself and as a parent realize that you are the best-qualified person in the world to take care of your little one.

As a doctor I had taken hundreds of exams to get to where I wanted to be. I could manage a sick baby confidently and competently, but throw me into something so normal as weaning and I was stumped. I looked for guidelines but mistook them for rules. I made mistakes and I followed others' leads as a path of least resistance. The truth is, I felt clueless and rudderless when it came to the transition to solids!

Despite my worries – and like most babies – my daughter fared fine during weaning, simply because I did the best that I could. Having children is a competitive sport. Try as you might not to compare yourself to others, you inevitably do. Everyone's child seems to be different to yours. Everyone's advice seems to be different to yours. Everyone's experience seems to be different to yours. Weaning is just another hurdle that you will jump like all the previous ones, in your own way and in your own time. The most important thing is that when the time comes to engage with this next baby phase you embrace it. It's a journey of excitement, exploration and experience, not just for baby but also for you. It doesn't have to be rushed or regimented, there are no major rules or rights or wrongs. It's an emotional journey because you are giving up a bit of control, but rest assured the rewards are immense. There is nothing quite like seeing a baby smile through a face full of spaghetti bolognese, it's priceless. My only regret is that I didn't take enough photographs. Get snap happy and record these precious moments.

In reality, weaning isn't a race. Don't be under pressure to start or stop. If in doubt, ask; most of the time you are doing the right thing but a bit of positive reassurance can go a long way. Enlist the help of others. It doesn't make you a bad parent if you don't home-make all the purées. It doesn't make you a better parent because you can boast your child has never fed from a jar. Instead, try to be the parent who enjoys weaning as much as your little one enjoys eating. Let the progression from mush to mash to mince be one messy adventure for you both!

Dr Pixie McKenna

"Weaning is
a journey
of excitement,
exploration and
experience."

"Weaning is a pivotal time in the life of both parent and child."

Introduction

Everyone has, at some point in their life, made the transition from liquids to solids, which by definition means they have been weaned. But what exactly does weaning mean? Weaning is the process through which an infant or any other young mammal becomes accustomed to food other than its mother's milk. The Americans tend to use the term weaning to specifically reference coming off the breast, as opposed to starting solids. You may even have heard the newer term 'complementary feeding' used. This book covers weaning as the transition from milk to first foods.

Weaning worries

Weaning is a pivotal time in the life of both parent and child. It constitutes a big developmental milestone signalling that your baby is maturing and making her way in life. Some parents are chomping at the bit for their baby to become independent of breast or bottle. Others may be more reticent about the weaning process, in particular those who are exclusively breast feeding as they may feel it might affect bonding. We rarely give as much thought to the psychological impact of weaning as we do the physical act of feeding. If you experience any feelings of anxiety, make sure you express them and enlist extra support as you wean – it's ok to have a wobble when faced with the decision to wean, it's normal. Rather than seeing it as giving something up, look at it as starting something new. Preparing for when you are going to wean, instead of suddenly deciding to go for it, will help you transition better. Set a date that suits, it doesn't have to be bang on 26 weeks. It's not set in stone, so don't rush it.

Ready for solids

Weaning is a rite of passage. It needs to be done around six months for practical reasons because baby is no longer getting what she nutritionally needs from breast or bottle alone. When your child is born she has an established supply of iron built up from her mum's supplies during pregnancy. By the 26-week mark, little baby has eaten into the iron overdraft so she needs to find a new source. In addition, the switch to solids starts working the muscles of the mouth and tongue, which will ultimately enable her to talk. Your baby is also developmentally ready to move on from milk as she is probably able to sit and hold her head at this age.

Start slow

It is important to transition into first foods smoothly and slowly. For the first few days you will panic that your baby isn't meeting her nutritional needs. Don't worry, in the initial stages it is more about how she engages than how much she ingests. Most of the food will end up on her face or the floor! This can be a bit deflating if you have spent hours painstakingly prepping baby's first ever dish. But once the first purées have been served up and swallowed, the path to lumpier and chunkier foods and ultimately family foods begins. Planning what foods you are going to introduce can make this transition a little smoother and really helps you feel in control, even when your baby has other ideas! It is not always easy to juggle everything, especially if you are working, but hopefully you will find that the recipes and example meal planners in this book can help you. Remember, every step of the way both you and your baby are experiencing and learning new things – enjoy it!

When to begin

When should you start weaning? Almost two decades ago it was normal to consider weaning at four months. However, in 2001, the World Health Organisation issued new guidelines stating that weaning should start at six months. The advice was that exclusive breast-feeding or formula feeding was adequate for all your baby's nutritional needs up this point and mums were advised to wait until 26 weeks before introducing purées. It's no wonder people are confused. Many parents would themselves have been weaned at four months and there is still baby food to cater for this age group on our supermarket shelves. The one firm rule is that you must not introduce your baby to first foods before 17 weeks.

Why wean?

The ultimate aim of weaning is to provide adequate nutrition and energy for your child, something he won't get from mother's milk or formula alone beyond six months. Weaning also plays an important role in the development of the muscles of mastication. These are the chewing muscles, which will help when the time comes for your little one to utter a few words. Weaning means a baby can experience new tastes and textures and develop social skills. The process fosters independence and makes your child feel like he belongs when he sits down and enjoys family food. Delaying weaning beyond six months may give rise to delays in the progression to solids and can have an impact on speech development. Nutritionally, the child may also miss out, with iron deficiency being a big concern in a late weaner. There is also a greater possibility of the child being a fussy eater if weaned late. But again, every child is different. Premature babies usually need to be weaned later than full-term babies to ensure they are ready for solids. Equally, children with cystic fibrosis have a high calorie demand and normally end up weaning earlier.

Signs to look out for

Your baby may be ready to begin weaning if he:

- can hold his head up. Your baby needs to be able to maintain an upright position in order to be able to swallow his food safely;

- has gained sufficient weight. As a guide, babies are often ready to be weaned when they have doubled their birth weight;

- makes chewing motions. If your baby starts to dribble less and can move food to the back of his mouth and swallow, he may be able to manage his first solid foods. If this skill has not been developed he will end up with more food around his mouth than in it;

- is curious about what you're eating. Watching you eating your meals and reaching out to try foods you're moving from your plate to your mouth is a key sign;

- has good co-ordination. Especially for baby-led weaning it is important that he should be able to look at food, grab it and put it in his mouth, all by himself.

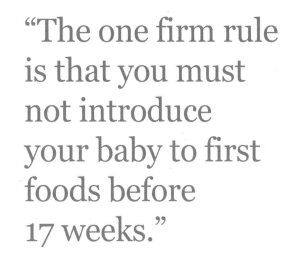

"The one firm rule is that you must not introduce your baby to first foods before 17 weeks."

Sometimes the following signs may seem indicative of your baby wanting to try food but often they can be common indicators for other things:

• Chewing fists – your baby may be teething.

• Waking in the night – he may be too hot or cold, or starting to crawl or walk.

• Increasing milk feeds – this could indicate a growth spurt or he may just be thirsty if the weather is hot.

Which weaning method to use

While you may have earmarked a date for the big departure to solids, have you decided how you are actually going to do it? In addition to the traditional, spoon-fed method, baby-led weaning is also an option. Baby-led weaning is not a new concept, in fact it's been around for about a decade. Neither is it a totally novel concept. Both methods have their advantages and disadvantages and I've outlined these below.

Traditional weaning

This method essentially introduces different types of puréed food to your baby using a soft spoon. Many parents start by introducing baby rice and move onto soft fruit and vegetable purées within the first few weeks. As your baby becomes comfortable with swallowing the purées, a courser texture can be introduced, followed by small lumps and finger foods at seven to nine months. The speed at which this progresses varies from baby to baby. There are some disadvantages with traditional weaning, such as that preparing purées can be time-consuming and may mean that your baby is eating a different meal from the rest of the family. She is also not learning about individual foods, tastes and textures when they are blended together. Parents often overfeed their children if they are in charge of the spoon. I've done it myself. Some parents may also spend too much time in the purée zone and delay progression to lumps, which can have a negative impact on oral development and speech further down the line, as well as lead to fussier eaters.

Baby-led weaning

Baby-led weaning follows a common-sense concept, where baby takes the lead to decide when, what and how much to eat. You obviously help by prepping the food and providing the venue and a routine. Baby can touch, taste, explore and eat foods at her own pace. While there is a technical risk of under eating, most texts will tell you that a baby will never starve when there's food around. It's a primitive instinct to fill up! However, baby-led weaning is not for you if you are a bit of a control freak. While ultimately you have little control when it comes to traditional weaning, allowing your baby to take control can prove quite stressful to the uninitiated. In addition you can't ensure your child is getting her iron quota if she's allowed to graze rather than be spoon fed.

Self feeding

Allowing your little one to take the lead helps her develop skills, gain independence and improve hand–eye co-ordination. Start by offering her soft finger foods at family meal times, so she can immediately socialize and mimic those around the table. Let her do her own spooning and get stuck in. As she is self feeding, she learns her hunger and satiety cues early on. Being in control now may mean she is less likely to be a picky eater in the future as she accepts a wide range of food. The flip side of this is you have no idea how much baby is actually eating. Many parents also have concerns about choking in self-feeders. Interestingly, a baby's gag reflex is further forward in the mouth than an adult's. She is hard wired to shoot something back out rather than suck it in. At six months, providing you offer appropriate foods, the choking risk should not be any greater with this method than if you spoon feed her.

The best method

Which method you decide to use is entirely up to you. Neither is incorrect. If you want, you can choose to take the best of both methods and wean your own way. Weaning should never be stressful for you or your baby. The best method is the one that works for you, not against you. Don't force yourself to do something that doesn't seem to fit with you – both approaches are guidelines, not law. The fundamental principal of weaning for me is knowing what you shouldn't do rather than dictating what you should. Just like baby finds her way through the purées, you too feel your way through weaning. The end goal is the same, the journey differs slightly for everyone.

"The best method is the one that works for you, not against you."

Stages 1 to 3

There is no definitive way to wean, just like there's no definitive way through pregnancy, teething or toilet training. As with any journey it's helpful to have a vague idea of where you are going, how long it's going to take and how you intend to get there. It's also good to have a steer for the dos and don'ts and an exit strategy for when things aren't going as planned. But that's the thing about babies – they are predictably unpredictable. They keep us on our toes long before they can stand on their own!

Stage 1

Very often, your baby's first serving is literally a spoonful of green gunk! His first taste is just that – a taste of things to come. Don't be surprised if he spits it straight back out. Remember this initial stage is less about the feeding and more about the taking part. The amount of calories consumed on day one will be negligible.

Stage 1 can be anything but should strictly be limited to one ingredient per purée, which is usually cooked then blended until completely smooth. If you need to soften it or make it smoother you can add expressed breast or formula milk, which will help to provide a familiar taste. If the purée tastes bland, resist the temptation to season it – salt is vetoed for this age group. Your baby should be fed with a spoon; ideally let him come to the spoon rather than bringing the spoon to him. If your first food choice is baby rice, mix it with milk as above. Resist the temptation to put it in the bottle as this poses a choking risk and doesn't encourage oral development.

The transition through the mushy phase involves offering a series of new options every two to three days. Offer veg first. Babies are hardwired to prefer sweet and salty foods so if you start with these,

you may struggle to get them enthusiastic about savoury foods. At the start, don't mix flavours together but gradually offer more individual flavours. Week one usually involves one daily offering of solids, week two has two offerings and by week three many will be on three 'meals' a day.

Stage 2

Most babies are on to stage 2 by seven months. The 'mash' menu is lumpier and firmer and has texture. Think potato or banana mashed with a fork rather than pulped. To start with you can mix a smooth purée with something chunkier for a familiar flavour. Finger foods can also be introduced at this stage. Your baby will be able to grasp things, so make the food in a shape he can pick up. Offer him soft finger foods like toast or cheese – you can see how exciting he finds it! Food shared is always a better dining experience so try to eat with him and encourage him. At this stage you can also advance him on to family foods like deconstructed spaghetti bolognaise (whizzed up but lumpy) so you can both eat off the same menu, just in different forms. Be cautious when prepping the food and make sure it's age appropriate in terms of the ingredients and additives.

Stage 3

Stage 3 foods are given at around nine to twelve months. Your baby is ready for food with a consistency of mince or chopped meat. Once again you are stepping up a gear in terms of texture, plus by now he has a few teeth to help tackle the food. The good news is that by the time he comes to the end of this phase he will be ready to enjoy full-on family food, albeit in smaller portions!

"Babies - they are predictably unpredictable."

First foods equipment

Before you start weaning, make sure you have all the staples. If you are weaning a six month old a high chair is a must. Try to get one with a removable tray so it can be washed straight after meals and put a big mat underneath to collect any dropped food. Invest in a range of bibs, ideally ones with sleeves and a little ledge at the end to catch the slops, and have lots of wet wipes and cleaning cloths to hand. The utensils are very important. Keep the colours bright and only use items that are suitable for babies. Get soft plastic spoons with a flat edge as they're easier for your baby to get the food off. In terms of how you should plate it up, I'm a fan of that thing that looks like a mish mash between a bowl and a saucer. It's the ultimate bit of baby crockery as it is multifunctional for everything from pasta to porridge to soup. It's plastic (so no damage, tick) it's flat (so it doesn't topple over, tick) and it has sides (so no spillages, tick). In my mind it's an essential.

Stage 1 weaning planner

And so you are off. While you will may be bursting with enthusiasm don't expect to get the same sentiment back from baby. You may be met with a disgruntled face and showered in spit. This stage is more about getting started than getting calories in. Remember you will still be breast- or bottle-feeding as normal until baby gets into her stride with solids. The first solids should be something savoury, not sweet. Baby rice is another option if you don't want to purée. Week one is an experimental week so keep the milk feeds as normal. Offer the first solids in the early evening and aim to offer them in the middle of the feed as baby isn't going to opt for solids if she's starving or full following a feed. Aim to introduce a new solid every two to three days. If she doesn't seem to like it on the first offering remember it can take 10–15 attempts before she decides it's palatable. In week one expect her to take one to six teaspoonfuls per meal.

If you find by week three that your baby is managing three sittings of solid food per day, it's time to progress to stage 2.

	Monday	Tuesday	Wednesday	Thursday	Friday	Saturday	Sunday
Wake Up	Milk	Milk	Milk	Milk	Milk	Milk	Milk
Mid Morning	Milk	Milk	Milk	Milk	Milk	Milk	Milk
Lunch	Milk – baby rice	Milk – carrot purée	Milk – sweet potato purée	Milk – pear purée	Milk – parsnip purée	Milk – baby rice and pea purée	Milk – apple purée
Mid Afternoon	Milk	Milk	Milk	Milk	Milk	Milk	Milk
Evening	Milk	Milk	Milk	Milk	Milk	Milk	Milk

Stage 2 weaning planner

At stage 2 we are stepping up from mush to mash. It's a much longer stage of weaning than stage 1. Get rid of the blender and instead hand mash with a fork for a lumpier texture. At this stage, baby begins not only to explore a greater variety of tastes and colours, but also to experience texture, flavour and food combinations. We want to broaden her horizons to avoid any fussy eating in the future. You can opt for stronger tasting foods like broccoli and cauliflower and sharper fruits like kiwis and plums. At this stage you can also start introducing finger foods. This can range from a rice cake to a cheese cube, just ensure they are soft enough for baby to chew or suck. You can also start adding soft cooked meat, pasta and rice to her repertoire. Aim for her to eat three lots of solids per day, reducing her milk feeds accordingly. You are ultimately trying to put a ceiling of 500–600 ml on milk consumption. Remember, however, the aim is not to come off milk entirely at this stage, but rather to complement it with solids. When introducing foods with allergy potential, do it one at a time. These foods include wheat, egg, mustard, peanut, seafood, sesame seeds and tree nuts such as almonds or hazelnuts. Wait for 72 hours before you trial your baby with a further potential allergen. Signs of a reaction include rash, vomiting, breathing difficulties and diarrhoea. None of these foods should be introduced before six months of weaning.

	Monday	Tuesday	Wednesday	Thursday	Friday	Saturday	Sunday
Wake Up	Milk	Milk	Milk	Milk	Milk	Milk	Milk
Breakfast	Spinach purée	Papaya and raspberry purée	Rice pudding	Kale purée	Banana and raspberry purée	Yogurt with stewed plums	Kiwi and banana purée
Mid Morning	Milk	Milk	Milk	Milk	Milk	Milk	Milk
Lunch	Milk – broccoli purée	Milk – lentil stew	Milk – chard purée	Milk – baked potato purée	Milk – cheesy broccoli purée	Milk – vegetable and brown rice gratin	Milk – squash and spinach risotto
Mid Afternoon	Melon and peach purée	Carrot and beef purée	Blueberry and banana purée	Chicken and cottage cheese	Salmon with peas and tomato	Rice pudding with mango	Sweet potato and chicken purée
Evening	Milk	Milk	Milk	Milk	Milk	Milk	Milk

Stage 3 weaning planner

The aim at stage 3 is to provide variety and nutrition while expanding the textures and flavours offered. Food at this stage can have lumps and chunks. Baby can now start to eat mince and chopped meats like lamb or beef. Finger food can be upgraded from soft to hard, e.g. toast. By this stage she has also mastered the pincer grasp so is able to pick up smaller morsels rather than rake them up. Take care when cutting up finger food to ensure it is cube shaped or baton shaped and avoid cutting things into coin shapes (e.g. slices of sausage) as this has a greater choking risk. You should be aiming to have baby eating three meals and two snacks a day by the end of this phase. This sounds like a lot but she will be moving around a great deal more than previously so she needs more calories. She will also be curious and keen to experience new things. When choosing foods, consider the iron content. This doesn't have to just be red meat – dried fruit, eggs, cereal and green veg are also great resources. Remember, to access iron for absorption you need vitamin C. Think of iron as the cash card and vitamin C as the pin. Fruit and veg are great vitamin C resources – mango, melon, tomato, even the humble potato!

	Monday	Tuesday	Wednesday	Thursday	Friday	Saturday	Sunday
Wake Up	Milk	Milk	Milk	Milk	Milk	Milk	Milk
Breakfast	Scrambled egg	Blueberry muffin	Omelette with bacon	Raisin and apple porridge	Blueberry porridge	Broccoli muffin	Eggy bread
Mid Morning	Tropical fruit yogurt	Spinach and cheese frittata	Prune porridge	Berry yogurt	Banana bread	Oat and honey biscuit	Raisin bun
Lunch	Chicken and courgette risotto	Cheesy pasta	Roast vegetable lasagne	Cheesy pasta with cauliflower	White fishcakes	Cheesy pasta with bacon	Carrot and broccoli risotto
Mid Afternoon	Milk	Milk	Milk	Milk	Milk	Milk	Milk
Dinner	Pea and carrot savoury pancakes	Chicken with vegetables and noodles	Kedgeree	Chicken fajitas	Spinach and ricotta pancakes	Turkey burger	Courgette and salmon couscous
Evening	Milk	Milk	Milk	Milk	Milk	Milk	Milk

Introducing first foods

When you're ready to wean, where do you start? Many people opt for baby rice. It's easy because it's ready made and involves far less mess than cooking up a purée storm in the kitchen. Mix it with breast or bottle milk, but never ever feed it to your baby straight from the bottle. Not only does this pose a choking risk, but as time goes on you need to curb his relationship with the bottle so he can learn how to chew his food. Offer veg first then fruit, initially individually, one at a time, in case of allergy, but you can mix and match as he builds up his repertoire. Hard fruit like apples must be stewed then puréed and everything must be peeled. When feeding, let your baby play and explore the spoon and the food. Encourage him to come to the spoon and only ever put the spoon in his mouth if it is open. He can also self-feed with his fingers. Some foods to avoid are listed below.

Salt

Babies under 12 months should have less than 1 gram of salt per day, as their kidneys are not sophisticated enough to deal with more. While you may not necessarily add salt to your food for seasoning, 80% of our daily salt intake is hidden. Beware the high salt content in stock cubes, sauces and processed foods, such as microwave meals. These are not suitable for babies.

Sugar

Sugar in food and drinks even at this early stage will lead to tooth decay in the future. It also paves the way for a sweet tooth, as many of our feeding habits are heavily engrained by the age of two years.

Honey

You should not add honey to sweeten food, use it as a glazing (for example, on ham) or use it to cover a soother to pacify a child under one year. This is because of the risk of botulin infection in children. Although rare, this infection can be fatal.

Nuts

Nuts should not be given to any children under five years due to the risk of choking. Ground nuts can be

given or children can eat nut butters if over the age of six months – just make sure that there is no family history of nut allergy.

Fish

Raw shellfish should be avoided for babies under the age of one year due to the risk of food poisoning. Marlin, shark and swordfish should also not be given due to the risk of mercury absorption, which can damage the nervous system.

Spices

Steer clear of hot spices like chilli. Milder spices such as coriander and cinnamon are fine in small quantities.

Other foods to avoid

Cows' milk must be avoided until the age of one year unless cooked into foods. Children under two years should also avoid low-fat foods, because fat is a resource of energy and certain vitamins in their diet. If weaned before six months, citrus fruits, liver, gluten, eggs and unpasteurized cheese should also be avoided.

First drinks

Your baby has spent the last six months drinking, so now it is time to cut back. From the age of six months he should drink from a cup or a free-flowing beaker. You want to get him out of the habit of sucking and into the habit of using his oral muscles to chew and swallow, which will help with speech development. Once you are happy that your baby is eating several times a day you can start to drop milk feeds. Your baby should be getting 500–600 ml of breast or formula milk per day once established on solids. While fruit juices can be given to children over six months I would not advise this, but if you must then limit them to meal times and dilute them one part juice to ten parts water. Avoid squash and other sugary drinks. If your baby is thirsty, give him water instead of milk. Before six months this must be boiled and cooled. Beware using bottled water as it may not be suitable for babies.

Preparing your purées

Making purées is fairly straightforward – you just take the individual fruit or veg and whizz it into a pulp. Even for a novice chef like me it seemed manageable. Making your own helps you get a better idea of taste and texture.

Purée prep

As with prepping any meal, good hygiene is very important – wash your hands before you start and make sure all your utensils are clean. If you are weaning your little one before 26 weeks, all utensils must be sterilized in a similar way to baby's bottles. All fruit and veg should be washed and peeled and hard fruits like apples must be boiled like veg. When mashing you can add formula or breast milk or simply use some of the cooking water. Do not season!

Storing purées

Once your fruit and veg is ready, use a stick blender to pulp it. Leave it to cool, then either refrigerate or freeze if you're not using it immediately. It's best to cook batches of food and freeze them in ice cube trays so you have a stash. Once frozen, the cubes can be removed from the tray and put into a freezer bag. Be sure you label and date the food clearly. I always stressed about batch freezing. I felt I was just being lazy, but as the time went on I realized it was a good option. While baby might lose out on some of the taste if you freeze their purée, the nutritional goodness remains intact so ease your conscience and freeze away! Make sure you defrost your foods at room temperature. If you take a shortcut and microwave defrost, you must consume the food immediately.

Heating food

Try not to use the microwave to warm baby food as you can't be sure it's evenly heated. It's preferable to warm it in a pan of hot water. If you must microwave, stir the food thoroughly once heated through to remove any hot spots. Check food is warmed right through by sticking a knife into it and testing the heat on the knife. Once you heat it you can reheat it once more, but after that it's time to bin it.

How long can I keep food in the freezer for?

- Cooked vegetable purées: 3–4 months

- Fruit purées: 6–12 months

- Cooked white fish: 4–6 months

- Oily fish (salmon, mackerel): 2–4 months

- Poultry: 4–6 months

- Cooked beef or lamb: 4–6 months

- Soups and sauces: 3–4 months

Stage 1
Recipes

Ready to get started? The recipes in this section are designed to be easy to prepare, so that you can relax and enjoy this phase of your child's development. To maximize the nutritional value of your purées, buy fresh or organic fruits and vegetables if possible and prepare within a day or two of purchasing.

The texture of the foods in this section should be semi-liquid purée. You'll find it easiest if you use a stick blender or food processor for puréeing, although it's fine to use whatever you have in your kitchen! Don't splash out where you don't need to – after all, this new stage has to suit your needs (and budget!), too.

Please be advised that some of the recipes in this section are only suitable for babies over eight months old.

Courgette purée

❄ Makes 6 portions and takes 20 minutes.

Courgettes are really easy to make into delicious baby food. Place 2 small courgettes (zucchinis) in a metal steaming basket over a small saucepan of boiling water, or cook in enough unsalted boiling water to just cover, for about 8–10 minutes until very soft. Drain, reserving a little cooking liquid.

Purée using a stick blender. Add 1–2 tbsp of the cooking water, formula or breast milk and mix to a thin, creamy consistency. Push through a fine sieve, then add more cooking water or milk to mix to the desired consistency. Serve lukewarm.

Sweet potato purée

❄ Makes 6 portions and takes 20 minutes.

This starchy, orange-coloured root vegetable is high in both calcium and potassium. To make a purée, peel and dice a small sweet potato. Place the sweet potato in a small saucepan of unsalted boiling water. Cook for 10 minutes until very soft. Drain, reserving a little cooking liquid.

Purée using a stick blender. Add 1–2 tbsp of the cooking liquid, formula or breast milk and mix to a thin, creamy consistency. Push through a fine sieve, then add more cooking water or milk to mix to the desired consistency. Serve lukewarm.

Parsnip purée

❄ *Makes 6 portions and takes 20 minutes.*

Parsnips are naturally sweet and high in fibre. Peel and dice 1 medium-sized parsnip and place the parsnip in a small saucepan of unsalted boiling water. Cook for 10 minutes until very soft. Drain, reserving a little cooking liquid.

Purée using a stick blender. Add 1–2 tbsp of the cooking liquid, formula or breast milk and mix to a thin, creamy consistency. Push through a fine sieve, then add more cooking water or milk to mix to the desired consistency. Serve lukewarm.

Potato purée

❄ *Makes 6 portions and takes 20 minutes.*

The humble potato has more potassium than a single banana and contains no sodium or cholesterol. Peel and dice a medium-sized potato. Place the potato in a small saucepan of unsalted boiling water. Cook for 10 minutes until very soft. Drain, reserving a little cooking liquid.

Purée using a stick blender. Add 1–2 tbsp of the cooking liquid, formula or breast milk and mix to a thin, creamy consistency. Push through a fine sieve, then add more cooking water or milk to mix to the desired consistency. Serve lukewarm.

Carrot purée

❄ *Makes 4 portions and takes 15 minutes.*

Deliciously sweet and succulent, carrots are incredibly versatile and a make for a healthy vitamin boost. As such, they are great first foods.

Peel and dice 2 carrots. Steam or boil the carrots in a saucepan over a medium heat for 10 minutes until completely tender. Purée using a stick blender. Add 3–4 tbsp of the cooking liquid, formula or breast milk to mix to a thin, creamy consistency. Serve lukewarm.

Pea purée

❄ *Makes 4 portions and takes 15 minutes.*

High in protein and fibre, peas are also a reliable source of omega 3.

Steam or boil 100 g / 3 ½ oz / ½ cup frozen peas in a saucepan over a medium heat for 5–8 minutes until very soft. Purée the peas using a stick blender, then pass the purée through a sieve to remove any skin or fibrous pieces. Thin again as required with boiled water, formula or breast milk. Serve lukewarm.

Green bean purée

❄ *Makes 4 portions and takes 15 minutes.*

Green beans contain a wealth of vitamins and minerals, especially high in folic acid and vitamin B.

Steam or boil 100 g / 3 ½ oz / ½ cup frozen green beans for 5–8 minutes until very soft. Purée the beans using a stick blender, then pass the purée through a sieve to remove any skin or fibrous pieces. Thin again as required with boiled water, formula or breast milk. Serve lukewarm.

Cauliflower purée

❄ *Makes 4 portions and takes 15 minutes.*

Cauliflower has a subtle flavour, but can be combined with sweet root vegetables to add variety.

Cut ⅓ small cauliflower into florets. Steam or boil for 8–10 minutes until very soft. Purée the cauliflower using a stick blender, then pass the purée through a sieve. Thin as desired with boiled water, formula or breast milk. Serve lukewarm.

Squash purée

❄ *Makes 4 portions and takes 15 minutes.*

Butternut squash is a healthy source of carbohydrate and antioxidant nutrients.

Chop, deseed and dice ¼ butternut squash. Steam or boil the squash in a small saucepan over a medium heat for about 15 minutes until tender. Purée using a stick blender. Add 1–2 tbsp of the cooking liquid, formula or breast milk and mix to a thin, creamy consistency. Push through a fine sieve, then add more cooking water or milk to mix to the desired consistency. Serve lukewarm.

Red pepper purée

❄ *Makes 2 portions and takes 15 minutes.*

The sweet taste of red peppers makes them an ideal early food for baby.

Preheat the grill. Wash, core and deseed a medium red pepper. Cut into quarters and roast under the grill until the skin is charred. Place the pepper in a plastic bag and allow to cool, then peel off the skin and purée to a smooth consistency. Serve immediately or cover and chill until needed.

Nectarine purée

❄ *Makes 4 portions and takes 10 minutes.*

Nectarines are naturally sweet and high in vitamin C. To make a purée, halve, stone and dice 1–2 ripe nectarines. Place the fruit into a small saucepan and add enough water to just cover.

Simmer for about 4–8 minutes until tender. Drain, reserving a little cooking liquid, then purée using a stick blender. Pass through a fine sieve to remove the pieces of skin. Thin with a little of the cooking water if necessary. Serve lukewarm.

Apricot purée

❄ *Makes 4 portions and takes 10 minutes.*

This soft summer fruit is delicious when in season. To make a purée, halve, stone and quarter 6 ripe apricots. Place the fruit into a small saucepan and add enough water to just cover.

Simmer for about 4–8 minutes until tender. Drain, reserving a little cooking liquid, then purée using a stick blender. Pass through a fine sieve to remove the pieces of skin. Thin with a little of the cooking water if necessary. Serve lukewarm.

Plum purée

❄ *Makes 4 portions and takes 10 minutes.*

Plums and prunes are packed with nutrients and promote good digestive health. Halve, stone and quarter 6 ripe plums. Place the fruit into a small saucepan and add enough water to just cover.

Simmer for about 4–8 minutes until tender. Drain, reserving a little cooking liquid, then purée using a stick blender. Pass through a fine sieve to remove the pieces of skin. Thin with a little of the cooking water if necessary. Serve lukewarm.

Apple purée

❄ *Makes 4 portions and takes 10 minutes.*

You could try adding a touch of cinnamon to this purée, once baby is accustomed to the apple taste. Peel, core and dice 1–2 dessert apples. Place the fruit into a small saucepan and add enough water to just cover.

Simmer gently for about 3–5 minutes until very soft. Drain, reserving a little cooking liquid. Purée using a stick blender, then pass through a fine sieve. Thin with a little of the cooking water if necessary. Serve lukewarm.

Top tip

Up until this stage, your baby has only consumed milk, which is sweet. As a result, she may be more interested in these lovely, fruity purées! Don't forget the importance of introducing plenty of savoury options, too.

Fresh fruits make delicious purées and are best when in season, but thawed frozen fruits are fine for puréeing, too. These purées can be made in batches and frozen in little portions, saving you time later!

Banana purée

Makes 4 portions and takes 5 minutes.

Bananas are deliciously creamy and high in potassium, making them an ideal ingredient for baby's first food! Their sweet flavour and mushy texture will go down a treat.

Peel and mash ½ ripe banana with a fork. Purée briefly with a stick blender, then mix the purée with a little formula or breast milk for a creamier consistency. Serve immediately.

Mango purée

Makes 4 portions and takes 5 minutes.

Low in saturated fat, cholesterol and sodium, mangoes are a sweet and refreshing fruit, perfect for your baby.

Peel one small ripe mango, remove the stone and chop the flesh. Purée using a stick blender until smooth, then thin with a little boiling water. Allow to cool, then serve.

Raspberry purée

Makes 4 portions and takes 5 minutes.

In the height of summer, raspberries are at their best. Use fresh or frozen raspberries in this refreshing recipe.

Pass 100 g / 3 ½ oz / 1 cup washed raspberries through a fine, non-metal sieve. Purée using a stick blender until smooth, then thin with a little boiling water. Allow to cool, then serve.

Barley porridge

Makes 3 portions and takes 10 minutes.

Barley is a good source of soluble fibre. Try mixing with a fruit purée for added flavour.

Place 50 g / 1 ¾ oz / ¼ cup whole barley into an electric grinder and process to a powder. Put 250 ml / 9 fl. oz / 1 cup water into a pan and bring to the boil. Add the barley powder and whisk well, then cover and simmer for about 10 minutes until cooked. Stir the mixture regularly. Purée using a stick blender, then add 3–4 tbsp of the cooking liquid, formula or breast milk to mix to the desired consistency. Serve lukewarm.

Oatmeal porridge

Makes 3 portions and takes 10 minutes.

Oats are easily digestible and a good, wholesome source of fibre, making them a great porridge for babies.

Place 25 g / 1 oz / ⅓ cup rolled oats into an electric grinder and process to a fine powder. Put 250 ml / 9 fl. oz / 1 cup water into a small pan and add the ground oats, mixing well. Bring to the boil, then simmer, stirring for 3–5 minutes. Allow to cool. Add formula or breast milk to thin to the desired consistency. Serve lukewarm.

Quinoa porridge

Makes 3 portions and takes 10 minutes.

Quinoa is rich in protein and is also gluten free. **This recipe is for babies over eight months old only.**

Place 70 g / 2 ½ oz / ⅓ cup quinoa in a sieve and rinse well, then drain. Place in a small pan with 160 ml / 6 fl. oz / ⅔ cup water and bring to the boil. Cover and simmer for about 12–15 minutes (or according to pack instructions) until the liquid is absorbed and the quinoa is soft. Blend the quinoa using a stick blender, then thin to desired consistency with formula or breast milk.

Stage 2
Recipes

Ready for lumps? The recipes in this section are designed for babies that have mastered the purée and are ready for chunkier textures and small lumps. The recipes may include dairy and gluten – check the ingredients list if your baby has an allergy to these types of foods.

Now that your little one is old enough to try a whole list of new foods, we have included some exciting and tasty recipes that are easy to prepare and store. At this stage, your baby is likely to be consuming 2–3 meals a day, so we've included recipes that are suitable for breakfast, lunch and dinner, to give you plenty of simple, nutritious options.

Spinach purée

❄ Makes 3 portions and takes 15 minutes.

Spinach is a great natural source of nutrients. To make a purée, wash 2 large handfuls of spinach leaves and cut out any tough stems, then chop roughly. Put into a pan and add a little water.

Cook for 3–5 minutes over a medium heat until wilted and tender. Drain, reserving the liquid, then purée using a stick blender. Thin to desired consistency with a little of the cooking water or mix into baby rice. Serve lukewarm.

Broccoli purée

❄ Makes 3 portions and takes 15 minutes.

If it's available, purple-sprouting broccoli makes a delicious alternative to this mighty green vegetable! To make a purée, steam or boil ½ small head of broccoli, cut into florets, in a saucepan of water over a medium heat for about 8 minutes until very tender.

Drain, reserving a little of the cooking liquid, then purée using a stick blender. Thin to desired consistency with a little of the cooking water. Serve lukewarm.

Chard purée

❄ Makes 3 portions and takes 15 minutes.

Different types of chard have different coloured stalks – look out for rainbow chard for a burst of colour in your kitchen! Wash 1 small bunch of chard leaves and cut out any tough stems, then chop roughly. Put into a pan and add a little water.

Cook for 3–5 minutes until wilted and tender. Drain, reserving the liquid, then purée using a stick blender. Thin to desired consistency with a little of the cooking water. Serve lukewarm.

Kale purée

❄ Makes 3 portions and takes 15 minutes.

Kale is available all year round but is best from September to February, making it a great seasonal winter vegetable. Wash 1 small bunch of organic kale and cut out any tough stems, then chop roughly. Put into a pan and add a little water.

Cook for 3–5 minutes until wilted and tender. Drain, reserving the liquid, then purée using a stick blender. Thin to desired consistency with a little of the cooking water. Serve lukewarm.

Sweet potato and chicken purée

 Makes 2 portions and takes 15 minutes.

Sweet potato and chicken are high in protein and carbohydrates. The sweet and savoury flavours in this purée make a delicious balanced meal.

¼ medium sweet potato, peeled and chopped

3 tbsp natural yogurt

¼ cooked chicken breast, finely chopped

- Steam or boil the sweet potato in a small pan for about 10 minutes until very tender.
- Drain, reserving a little of the cooking liquid, then purée the sweet potato using a stick blender.
- Add the yogurt and chicken and blend briefly to a coarse purée. Add a little of the cooking water to thin to the desired consistency. Serve lukewarm.

Carrot and beef purée

 Makes 2 portions and takes 25 minutes.

Beef is a good source of protein and iron, which is important for your baby's diet at this stage in his development. It's also easily digestible, making it a great ingredient for purées.

2 tsp sunflower oil

1 small carrot, peeled and grated

100 g / 3 ½ oz / ½ cup lean minced beef

1 tomato, chopped

80 ml / 3 fl. oz / ⅓ cup low-sodium vegetable stock

- Heat the oil in a small pan. Add the carrot and cook for 2–3 minutes. Add the minced beef, tomato and stock and bring to the boil, stirring. Cover and simmer gently for 15–20 minutes.
- Remove from the heat and purée to a coarse consistency using a stick blender. Add a little more stock if necessary to thin to the desired consistency. Serve lukewarm.

Top tip

Stage 2 purées can be a little chunkier than the almost-liquid blends from stage 1. You can mash the ingredients with a fork, rather than a stick blender, to achieve a thicker, lumpier consistency.

You can also now introduce meats to baby's diet, providing important proteins and iron that are vital for his development.

Vegetable and brown rice gratin

 Makes 2 portions and takes 50 minutes.

60 g / 2 oz / ¼ cup brown rice

200 ml / 7 fl. oz / ¾ cup low-sodium
    vegetable stock

25 g / 1 oz / ⅛ cup carrot

25 g / 1 oz / ⅛ courgette (zucchini)

25 g / 1 oz / ⅛ cup red pepper

25 g / 1 oz / ¼ cup Cheddar cheese,
    finely grated

• Wash the rice well under cold water. Place the stock into a small
  pan and bring to the boil. Add the rice, stir and bring back to the boil.
  Cover tightly and simmer very gently for about 30 minutes until the
  rice is cooked.

• Finely chop the vegetables, then add to the pan with a little more
  stock if necessary. Cover and simmer for 10 minutes.

• Remove from the heat and mash or purée to a coarse texture.
  Add more stock or boiled water if necessary to reach the desired
  consistency. Sprinkle with cheese and serve lukewarm.

Squash and spinach risotto

 Makes 2 portions and takes 50 minutes.

⅛ small butternut squash, peeled
    deseeded and chopped

2 tsp sunflower oil

¼ small onion, finely chopped

55 g / 2 oz / ¼ cup risotto rice

350 ml / 12 fl. oz / 1 ½ cups low-sodium
    vegetable stock

handful baby spinach leaves

2 tsp Parmesan cheese, grated

• Steam or boil the butternut squash for 10–15 minutes or until tender.
  Purée or mash with a fork. Heat the sunflower oil in a small pan and
  add the onion, then cook for about 5 minutes until soft.

• Add the rice to the pan and cook for 1 minute. Slowly incorporate the
  stock, then cook over a medium to low heat for about 15 minutes
  until the stock is absorbed and the rice is cooked. Add the spinach
  leaves and stir until wilted.

• Stir in the squash purée and the Parmesan, then purée or mash the
  risotto to a course texture. Add a little more stock if necessary to
  reach the desired consistency. Serve lukewarm.

Lentil stew

 Makes 2 portions and takes 30 minutes.

50 g / 1 ¾ oz / ¼ cup dried split
    red lentils

½ small potato, peeled and diced

1 small carrot, peeled and diced

2 tbsp coconut milk or natural yogurt

• Put the lentils and potato into a small pan and cover with water.
  Bring to the boil, then reduce the heat. Add the carrot and simmer
  for 15–20 minutes until tender, adding more water if necessary.

• Drain, reserving some of the cooking liquid. Return the lentils
  and vegetables to the pan, then stir in the coconut milk or yogurt
  and a little of the cooking liquid. Mash or purée to the desired
  consistency. Serve lukewarm.

Turkey and parsnip purée

 Makes 3 portions and takes 30 minutes.

This nourishing purée is ideal for the cold winter months. Greek yogurt will provide your baby with plenty of calcium and is great for the immune system, while turkey is packed with protein and essential iron for your baby's growth.

150 g / 5 oz / ½ cup skinless turkey breast, diced or minced

1 small parsnip, peeled and diced

250 ml / 9 fl. oz / 1 cup low-sodium chicken stock

1–2 tbsp natural Greek yogurt

- Put all the ingredients except the yogurt into a small pan. Bring to the boil. Cover and reduce to a simmer, then cook for about 20 minutes until tender.
- Using a stick blender, process to a coarse purée. Thin to the desired consistency with a little stock. Stir in the yogurt. Serve lukewarm.

Baked potato purée

 Makes 2 portions and takes 50 minutes.

Potatoes work well as a base ingredient and can be combined with other root vegetables, cheeses or cooked meat for variety. They're a good source of carbohydrates, which your baby needs in her diet.

1 small baking potato

olive oil, for rubbing

- Heat the oven to 200°C (180°C fan) / 400F / gas 6. With a knife, make an incision around the potato halfway up. Rub the potato with a little olive oil and place on a baking tray. Bake for 30–45 minutes depending on size.
- Cut the potato in half and spoon the flesh into a bowl. Add formula or breast milk to mix to a soft consistency. Add grated cheese or puréed vegetables to the potato as desired. Serve lukewarm.

Cheesy broccoli purée

 Makes 2 portions and takes 20 minutes.

This green power vegetable is packed with plenty of nutritional goodness, including vitamin D and fibre. Combined with cheese, this simple purée contains a heap of flavour that your baby will love, as well as being nutritionally balanced.

3 broccoli florets

1 tbsp butter

1 tbsp plain (all-purpose) flour

150 ml / 5 fl. oz / ⅔ cup full-fat milk

2 tbsp Cheddar cheese, finely grated

- Steam or boil the broccoli until tender, then drain.
- Melt the butter in a small pan, then stir in the flour and cook for 30 seconds. Remove from the heat and add the milk slowly. Return to the heat, stirring continuously until the sauce has thickened.
- Remove from the heat and add the cheese. Mash, finely chop or purée the cooked broccoli, then stir into the sauce. Thin with a little more milk to reach the desired consistency. Serve lukewarm.

Chicken and cottage cheese

Makes 2 portions and takes 5 minutes.

Rich in both calcium and selenium, cottage cheese supports immune system function. Both of these vital elements encourage strong bone development, making them perfect for your baby!

¼ cooked skinless, boneless chicken breast

3 tbsp cottage cheese

1 tbsp natural yogurt

- Chop the chicken breast as small as possible or use a stick blender. Mix together the chicken, cottage cheese and yogurt. Mash with a fork or purée to the desired consistency.

Carrot and tomato with lentils

 Makes 3 portions and takes 20 minutes.

Lentils are a great source of insoluble fibre, which promotes healthy digestion. They can be bought pre-cooked or in their original dry, un-cooked state. If using dried lentils in this recipe, you can soak them overnight in order to reduce cooking time.

50 g / 1 ¾ oz / ¼ cup dried split red lentils

1 carrot, peeled and chopped

1–2 tsp tomato purée

- Put the lentils and carrot into a small pan and cover with water. Bring to the boil, then reduce the heat and simmer for about 10 minutes until tender.
- Stir in the tomato purée and cook for 1–2 minutes. Drain, reserving any cooking liquid. Purée using a stick blender, then add a little of the cooking water to mix to the desired consistency. Serve lukewarm.

Salmon with peas and tomato

 Makes 4 portions and takes 50 minutes.

Packed with vitamins, minerals and omega 3 fats, salmon is both tasty and nutrient dense. It absorbs flavours nicely and works beautifully with fresh or frozen garden peas.

sunflower oil, for brushing

1 small skinless, boneless salmon fillet

1 small potato, peeled and diced

2 tbsp frozen peas

1 tsp tomato purée

4–5 tbsp formula or breast milk

- Heat the oven to 190°C (170°C fan) / 375F / gas 5. Place a square of foil on a baking tray and brush with a little sunflower oil.
- Place the salmon fillet in the centre and spoon over 2 tsp water. Gather up the edges of the foil to make a parcel. Bake in the oven for 20–30 minutes until the fish is cooked through.
- Steam or boil the potato and peas for 7–10 minutes until tender.
- Drain, then mash, chop or purée the potatoes and peas in a bowl. Add the salmon, tomato purée and milk and mash well together with a fork or stick blender. Serve lukewarm.

Papaya and raspberry smoothie

Makes 4 portions and takes 5 minutes.

1 papaya, peeled, deseeded and diced
handful raspberries, washed
pure apple juice, to mix

• Put the papaya and raspberries into a food processor and blend until smooth. Pass through a sieve. Thin to the desired consistency with a little apple juice. Serve immediately.

Banana and raspberry smoothie

Makes 4 portions and takes 5 minutes.

1 small ripe banana
handful raspberries, washed
natural yogurt, to mix

• Put the banana and raspberries into a food processor and blend until smooth. Sieve, then stir in natural yogurt to mix to reach the desired consistency. Serve immediately.

Kiwi and banana smoothie

Makes 4 portions and takes 5 minutes.

1 small kiwi fruit
1 small banana
natural yogurt, to mix

• Peel and chop the kiwi fruit, then purée together with the banana and mix with natural yogurt in a food processor to reach the desired consistency. Serve immediately.

Top tip

Food processors are great tools for mashing up baby foods! They have more functions and speeds than a blender, which means you have more control over the consistency of your purées.

If you don't have a food processor, a stick blender will work just fine for these fruity concoctions!

Rice pudding

Makes 3 portions and takes 30 minutes.

Grains are incredibly versatile and can be introduced into the weaning diet fairly early. They have great nutritional value, and this sweet dish will help to bridge the gap between milk and solids.

50 g / 1 ¾ oz / ¼ cup short-grain pudding rice

500 ml / 18 fl. oz / 2 cups full-fat milk

¼ tsp vanilla extract

2 tsp sugar (optional)

- Put the rice, milk, vanilla extract and sugar, if using, into a small pan.
- Bring to the boil and simmer very gently for about 25 minutes, stirring frequently.
- When the rice is very soft, remove from the heat and leave to cool. Thin as necessary with more milk. Serve lukewarm.

Rice pudding with mango

Makes 3 portions and takes 30 minutes.

Adding fruits to rice pudding is a great way to liven up this dish, and it incorporates a heap of nutritional value, too. Babies love the sweetness of fruit, so this tropical addition will be a hit!

50 g / 1 ¾ oz / ¼ cup short-grain pudding rice

500 ml / 18 fl. oz / 2 cups full-fat milk

¼ tsp vanilla extract

1 small ripe mango

- Put the rice, milk and vanilla extract into a small pan.
- Bring to the boil and simmer very gently for about 25 minutes, stirring frequently.
- Peel and stone the mango and purée the flesh using a stick blender.
- When the rice is very soft, remove from the heat and leave to cool, then stir in the mango purée. Thin as necessary with more milk. Serve lukewarm.

Yogurt with stewed plums

 Makes 3 portions and takes 15 minutes.

This simple recipe can be prepared in minutes and enjoyed at any time. The silky smooth texture will provide relief to little ones who are teething, simply by cooling and soothing the gums.

6 ripe plums, pitted and quartered

2–3 tbsp apple juice

3 tbsp natural Greek yogurt

- Put the plums and apple juice into a small pan, then cover and simmer gently for 10–15 minutes until the plums are very soft.
- Purée with a stick blender. Pass the purée through a fine sieve to remove any skin. Add cooled, boiled water to reach the desired consistency.
- Serve alongside or mixed into the yogurt.

Semolina with blueberries

 Makes 2 portions and takes 15 minutes.

This recipe would work well with any berries – why not try strawberries or blackberries when they're in season?

handful of blueberries

250 ml / 9 fl. oz / 1 cup full-fat milk

2 tbsp semolina

- Put the blueberries and a splash of water into a small pan. Heat gently until boiling and stir for a couple of minutes. Remove from the heat, then roughly crush the berries using the back of a spoon. Put to one side.
- Heat the milk in a small pan. Add the semolina and cook for 3–5 minutes, stirring frequently, until the desired consistency is reached. Add a little more milk if necessary, then leave to cool.
- Serve the semolina topped with the blueberries.

Ricotta with raspberries

 Makes 3 portions and takes 5 minutes.

This creamy dish makes a fun dessert for baby, but is also something the whole family can enjoy.

120 g / 4 oz / 1 cup raspberries

2 tbsp boiled, cooled water

3 tbsp full-fat ricotta cheese

- Put the raspberries and water into a small bowl. Purée using a stick blender, then pass through a fine sieve to remove seeds.
- Layer the ricotta and raspberry purée in little cups and serve.

Apple and raspberry custard

 Makes 3 portions and takes 35 minutes.

1 dessert apple, peeled, cored and
finely chopped

60 g / 2 oz / ½ cup raspberries, lightly
crushed with a fork

2 egg yolks, beaten

250 ml / 9 fl. oz / 1 cup full-fat milk

- Heat the oven to 180°C / 160°C fan / 350F / gas 4.
- Mix together the apple and raspberries and place in the bottom of a small baking dish.
- Whisk together the egg yolks and the milk and pour over the fruit. Place the dish in a small baking tin and pour in enough hot water to come halfway up the sides of the dish.
- Bake in the oven for about 20–30 minutes until set. Allow to cool before serving.

  NOTE: Not suitable for babies under eight months.

Fig and nectarine purée

 Makes 3 portions and takes 10 minutes.

1 ripe nectarine, peeled, halved, stoned
and diced

2 ripe figs, peeled and quartered

- Purée the nectarine with a stick blender or mash with a fork.
- Purée the figs with a stick blender, then mix the two purées together. Thin with a little pure apple juice or cooled boiled water if necessary. Serve immediately.

Melon and peach purée

Makes 3 portions and takes 10 minutes.

1 ripe peach, peeled, halved, stoned
and diced

1 wedge of gala or cantaloupe melon

- Purée the peach with a stick blender or mash well with a fork.
- Remove the skin and seeds from the melon and purée with a stick blender. Mix the two purées together and serve immediately.

Blueberry and banana purée

 Makes 2 portions and takes 10 minutes.

50 g / 2 oz / ½ cup blueberries

2 tbsp water

2 small ripe bananas, peeled and chopped

- Put the blueberries in a saucepan with the water and cook for 5 minutes.
- Remove the pan from the heat. Add the chopped banana to the pan and blend with a stick blender to the desired consistency.
- Serve lukewarm or cover and chill until needed.

Apple and blackberry purée

Makes 2 portions and takes 15 minutes.

1 dessert apple, peeled, cored and chopped

a handful of fresh or frozen blackberries

2 tbsp water

- Put the apple, blackberries and water into a small pan. Bring almost to the boil, then cover.
- Reduce the heat to low and cook gently for about 8 minutes until the fruit is very soft. Stir from time to time adding more water if necessary. Purée with a stick blender, then serve lukewarm.

Pear and apricot purée

Makes 2 portions and takes 15 minutes.

1 ripe pear, peeled, cored and chopped

6 ready-to-eat dried apricots

3–4 tbsp water

- Put the pear, apricots and water into a small pan. Bring almost to the boil, then cover.
- Reduce the heat to low and cook gently for about 8 minutes until the fruit is very soft. Stir from time to time adding more water if necessary. Purée with a stick blender, then serve lukewarm.

Top tip

Don't worry if the portion sizes given with the recipes don't exactly match what your baby is eating. All babies are different, and you will find that the amount of food needed to maintain their growth rate varies from one baby to the next. The amount your baby eats may also vary from week to week – this is normal.

The main thing is that your baby is having a healthy diet over the course of a week.

Stage 3
Recipes

Ready to solidify? The recipes in this section are designed to introduce more substantial foods and sophisticated flavours, now that your baby is almost ready for solids. You can finally banish the blender as she tackles these delicious meals!

Now that your little one is getting to grips with chewing, she may even be feeding herself and eager to enjoy the same meals as you! Many of the recipes in this section are suitable for the whole family, so that you won't need to prepare several dishes at mealtimes and can optimize your time in the kitchen.

Scrambled egg

Makes 2 portions and takes 10 minutes.

This quick and tasty breakfast classic can be eaten with some healthy wholemeal toast cut into little squares for child-friendly portions.

knob of butter

2 eggs, lightly beaten

2 tbsp full-fat milk

¼ tsp parsley or chives, finely chopped

- Heat the butter in a small pan. Beat together the eggs and milk.
- When the butter is melted, stir in the eggs. Cook over a low heat, stirring and folding the eggs continuously until well cooked and scrambled. Stir in the parsley or chives and serve with toast.

NOTE: Not suitable for babies under ten months.

Omelette with bacon

Makes 2 portions and takes 10 minutes.

This omelette will provide your child with plenty of energy to see her through to lunch. For a protein-rich vegetarian version, omit the bacon and replace with some grated cheese.

knob of butter

2 eggs, beaten

1 tsp water

1 rasher cooked unsmoked back bacon, finely chopped

- Melt the butter in a small non-stick frying pan.
- Beat the eggs with the water and stir in the bacon. Pour the mixture into the pan and swirl around to cover the base.
- Cook over a medium heat for about 2 minutes until it has set, then turn the omelette over and cook for a further minute or so.
- Turn out onto a plate and slice into child-friendly pieces.

NOTE: Not suitable for babies under ten months.

Eggy bread

Makes 2 portions and takes 10 minutes.

Serve alongside grilled cup mushrooms, iron-rich greens and cherry tomatoes for a healthy meal.

1 egg

1 tbsp full-fat milk

1 slice thick white or brown bread

knob of butter

1 tsp olive oil

- Beat the egg and milk together. Lay the bread in a shallow dish and pour over the egg mixture. Turn the bread over to coat all over.
- Heat the butter and oil in a small non-stick frying pan over a medium heat. Add the soaked bread and cook for about 2 minutes until the underside is golden brown.
- Flip the bread over and cook for another couple of minutes until golden brown. Cut into fingers to serve.

NOTE: Not suitable for babies under ten months.

Mini blueberry muffins

❄ *Makes 12 mini muffins and takes 30 minutes.*

These sweet blueberry muffins can be eaten at any time and are delicious served warm. Your baby can now consume whole fruits, so the blueberries in this recipe provide a lovely burst of flavour.

1 large egg

125 ml / 4 ½ fl. oz / ½ cup full-fat milk

4 tbsp sunflower oil

**200 g / 7 oz / 1 ½ cups plain
(all-purpose) flour**

2 tsp baking powder

**100 g / 3 ½ oz / ½ cup caster
(superfine) sugar**

handful small blueberries

- Heat oven to 200°C (180°C fan) / 400F / gas 6. Place 12 mini cake cases in a muffin tin.
- Beat the egg, then whisk in the milk and oil. Sieve the flour and baking powder into a bowl. Stir in the sugar, then add the blueberries.
- Add the egg mixture and stir just until the flour is mixed in – don't over-mix or the mixture will be heavy.
- Fill the muffin cases two-thirds full. Bake in the oven for about 15 minutes until risen and golden brown.

Mini broccoli muffins

❄ *Makes 12 mini muffins and takes 25 minutes.*

These savoury muffins make ideal snacks or a tasty lunchtime treat to accompany a salad or soup. They're also a friendly size for little ones, who need to get their mitts on plenty of finger foods at this stage to help them develop.

150 g / 5 oz / 1 cup self-raising flour

½ tsp baking powder

**2 broccoli florets, cooked and finely
chopped**

2 tbsp Cheddar cheese, grated

**50 g / 1 ¾ oz / ¼ cup butter,
melted and cooled**

125 ml / 4 ½ fl. oz / ½ cup milk

1 egg, lightly beaten

- Heat the oven to 190°C (170°C fan) / 375F / gas 5. Put 12 mini muffin cases into a mini muffin tray.
- Sieve together the flour and baking powder, then stir in the broccoli and cheese.
- Beat together the butter, milk and egg and add to the flour mixture. Stir until just combined.
- Spoon into the prepared cases and bake for about 10 minutes until risen and golden brown.

Tropical fruit yogurt

Makes 2 portions and takes 10 minutes.

¼ ripe mango, peeled and chopped

¼ ripe papaya, peeled and chopped

½ small ripe banana

200 g / 7 oz / ¾ cup natural Greek yogurt

- Purée the mango, papaya and banana using a stick blender, then sieve to remove any seeds.
- Divide the purée between two small dishes. Spoon the yogurt on top and serve.

Berry yogurt

Makes 2 portions and takes 10 minutes.

180 g / 6 oz / 1 cup mixed berries (raspberries, blackberries, blueberries)

200 g / 7 oz / ¾ cup natural Greek yogurt

- Purée the berries using a stick blender, then sieve to remove any seeds.
- Divide the purée between two small dishes. Spoon the yogurt on top and serve.

Top tip

These yogurts are great little breakfasts or snacks for children. They're packed with fruity flavour, plus a helping of calcium to help bones grow nice and strong!

Following the above recipes, why not experiment with other fruit flavours? Substituting these fruits for your baby's favourites will go down a treat!

Raisin and apple porridge

Makes 3 portions and takes 10 minutes.

This delicious oaty porridge is full of fruity flavours that your baby will now be familiar with. Why not sprinkle a little cinnamon on top before serving, or stir into the porridge to add a new depth of flavour.

40 g / 1 ½ oz / ⅓ cup porridge oats

300 ml / 11 fl. oz / 1 ⅓ cups full-fat milk

1 small dessert apple

1 tbsp raisins, roughly chopped

- Put the oats and milk into a small pan and bring to the boil. Reduce heat and simmer for about 5 minutes, stirring frequently until the oats are cooked.
- Peel, core and coarsely grate the dessert apple. Stir the raisins and apple into the cooked porridge. Heat for 1–2 minutes, adding a little more milk if necessary. Cool before serving lukewarm.

Blueberry porridge

Makes 3 portions and takes 10 minutes.

Porridge is a simple dish that can be spruced up with any of your baby's favourite fruits. Plus, this makes a great breakfast for the whole family, meaning that you can cater for everyone with one easy and nutritious dish!

40 g / 1 ½ oz / ⅓ cup porridge oats

300 ml / 11 fl. oz / 1 ⅓ cups full-fat milk

handful blueberries

- Put the oats and milk into a small pan and bring to the boil. Reduce heat and simmer for about 5 minutes, stirring frequently until the oats are cooked.
- Add the blueberries and mash them into the porridge. Heat for 1–2 minutes, adding a little more milk if necessary. Cool before serving lukewarm.

Prune porridge

Makes 3 portions and takes 10 minutes.

Porridge is a fantastic way to get a good dose of dairy into your baby's diet – remember that for the first two years she needs full-fat milk, so avoid semi-skimmed or other low-fat varieties.

40 g / 1 ½ oz / ⅓ cup porridge oats

300 ml / 11 fl. oz / 1 ⅓ cups full-fat milk

6 dried prunes, pitted

- Put the oats and milk into a small pan and bring to the boil. Reduce heat and simmer for about 5 minutes, stirring frequently until the oats are cooked.
- Roughly chop the prunes and stir into the porridge. Heat for 1–2 minutes, adding a little more milk if necessary. Cool before serving lukewarm.

Raisin buns

 Makes 8 buns and takes 2 hours, including time to rise.

Enjoy these raisin buns with some home-made fruit jam and fresh cream for a delicious treat, or simply top with a little butter. Make a batch of these buns for the whole family!

250 ml / 9 fl. oz / 1 cup full-fat milk

1 tbsp dried active yeast

500 g / 18 oz / 4 cups plain
(all-purpose) flour

50 g / 1 ¾ oz / ¼ cup caster (superfine)
sugar

50 g / 1 ¾ oz / ¼ cup butter,
melted and cooled

1 egg, beaten

100 g / 3 ½ oz / ½ cup raisins

- Heat the milk in a small saucepan until just lukewarm, then stir in the yeast.
- Put the flour and sugar into a bowl and mix together. Stir in the milk, butter and egg and mix until the mixture is soft but not sticky. Add the raisins and knead into the dough.
- Place the mixture into a clean bowl, cover with cling film and leave to rise in a warm place for about 1 hour, until doubled in size.
- Turn the dough out onto a lightly floured board and knead until smooth. Cut into eight and shape into balls. Place in a non-stick muffin tin or lined individual metal cups. Leave to rise in a warm place for about 30 minutes.
- Heat the oven to 200°C (180°C fan) / 400F / gas 6. Bake the buns in the oven for 15–20 minutes until well risen and golden brown.

Top tip

Now that your little one can eat whole fruits, try different flavours in these buns such as cherries with the pits removed, banana slices, blueberries or chopped apricots.

These can be stored for up to a week in an airtight container – although they'll prove to be so popular that they might not last that long!

Pancakes with fruit

 Makes 12 pancakes and takes 30 minutes.

170 g / 6 oz / 1 ⅓ cups plain
(all-purpose) flour

1 ½ tsp baking powder

1 large egg

180 ml / 6 fl. oz / ¾ cup full-fat milk

1 tbsp butter, melted

sunflower oil, for cooking

handful seedless green grapes, halved

handful seedless red grapes, halved

- Sieve the flour and baking powder into a bowl and make a well in the centre.
- Whisk together the egg and milk and stir in the butter. Pour the egg mixture into the flour gradually and whisk to a smooth batter.
- Heat 2 tsp oil in a non-stick frying pan over a medium heat. Add 2 tbsp of the batter per pancake. Cook each pancake for about 2 minutes each side. Remove and keep warm.
- Serve the pancakes with the grapes. If over 12 months, drizzle a little honey over the pancakes.

Pancakes with banana and syrup

 Makes 12 pancakes and takes 30 minutes.

170 g / 6 oz / 1 ⅓ cups plain
(all-purpose) flour

1 ½ tsp baking powder

1 large egg

180 ml / 6 fl. oz / ¾ cup full-fat milk

1 tbsp butter, melted

sunflower oil, for cooking

1 large banana, sliced

maple syrup, to serve

- Sieve the flour and baking powder into a bowl and make a well in the centre.
- Whisk together the egg and milk and stir in the butter. Pour the egg mixture into the flour gradually and whisk to a smooth batter.
- Heat 2 tsp oil in a non-stick frying pan over a medium heat. Add 2 tbsp of the batter per pancake. Cook each pancake for about 2 minutes each side. Remove and keep warm.
- Serve the pancakes topped with banana slices and a drizzle of maple syrup.

Waffles with strawberry purée

 Makes 6 portions and takes 10 minutes.

250 g / 9 oz / 1 cup strawberries,
hulled and halved

50 g / 1 ¾ oz / ¼ cup caster (superfine)
sugar

2 tbsp water

2 tsp cornflour (cornstarch)

waffles, to serve

- Mash the strawberries in a bowl, then put them into a small pan with the sugar, water and cornflour. Stir over a medium heat until boiling and thickened.
- Reduce the heat to low and cook gently, stirring continuously, for 30 seconds. Serve with waffles or pancakes.

Chicken and courgette risotto

 Makes 2 portions and takes 30 minutes.

¼ chicken breast, cooked and shredded

1 shallot, finely chopped

½ courgette (zucchini), chopped

80 g / 3 oz / ⅓ cup long grain rice

200 ml / 7 fl. oz / ¾ cup low-sodium
vegetable stock or water

- Put all the ingredients into a small pan and bring to the boil.
- Reduce the heat, cover and simmer for 20 minutes until the rice is tender and the liquid is absorbed. Add a little more stock or water if necessary.
- Serve, or purée to the desired texture with a stick blender.

Pea and mint risotto

 Makes 2 portions and takes 30 minutes.

4 tbsp frozen peas

1 shallot, finely chopped

6 mint leaves, chopped

80 g / 3 oz / ⅓ cup long grain rice

200 ml / 7 fl. oz / ¾ cup low-sodium
vegetable stock or water

- Put all the ingredients into a small pan and bring to the boil.
- Reduce the heat, cover and simmer for 20 minutes until the rice is tender and the liquid is absorbed. Add a little more stock or water if necessary.
- Serve, or purée to the desired texture with a stick blender.

Carrot and broccoli risotto

 Makes 2 portions and takes 30 minutes.

1 small carrot, peeled and coarsely
grated

1 shallot, finely chopped

1 broccoli floret, chopped

80 g / 3 oz / ⅓ cup long grain rice

200 ml / 7 fl. oz / ¾ cup low-sodium
vegetable stock or water

- Put all the ingredients into a small pan and bring to the boil.
- Reduce the heat, cover and simmer for 20 minutes until the rice is tender and the liquid is absorbed. Add a little more stock or water if necessary.
- Serve, or purée to the desired texture with a stick blender.

Cheesy pasta

 Makes 1 portion and takes 20 minutes.

1 tsp butter

2 tsp cornflour (cornstarch)

150 ml / 5 fl. oz / ⅔ cup full-fat milk

50 g / 1 ¾ oz / ½ cup Cheddar cheese, grated

50 g / 1 ¾ oz / ½ cup macaroni, or other small pasta

- Put the butter, cornflour and milk into a small pan. Heat gently, then bring to the boil, stirring constantly. When the sauce has thickened, add the cheese.
- Cook the pasta according to pack instructions. Drain and stir into the cheese sauce. Serve, or purée to the desired consistency.

Cheesy pasta with bacon

 Makes 1 portion and takes 20 minutes.

1 tsp butter

2 tsp cornflour (cornstarch)

150 ml / 5 fl. oz / ⅔ cup full-fat milk

50 g / 1 ¾ oz / ½ cup Cheddar cheese, grated

50 g / 1 ¾ oz / ½ cup macaroni, or other small pasta

1 rasher streaky bacon

- Put the butter, cornflour and milk into a small pan. Heat gently, then bring to the boil, stirring constantly. When the sauce has thickened, add the cheese.
- Cook the pasta according to packet instructions. While the pasta is cooking, grill the bacon until crispy. Once the pasta is ready, drain and stir into the cheese sauce. Serve, or purée to the desired consistency.
- Crumble or chop the bacon rasher and stir into the macaroni cheese just before serving.

Cheesy pasta with cauliflower

 Makes 1 portion and takes 20 minutes.

1 tsp butter

2 tsp cornflour (cornstarch)

150 ml / 5 fl. oz / ⅔ cup full-fat milk

50 g / 1 ¾ oz / ½ cup Cheddar cheese, grated

50 g / 1 ¾ oz / ½ cup macaroni, or other small pasta

1–2 cauliflower florets

- Put the butter, cornflour and milk into a small pan. Heat gently, then bring to the boil, stirring constantly. When the sauce has thickened, add the cheese.
- Cook the pasta according to packet instructions. While the pasta is cooking, steam or boil the cauliflower. Once the pasta is ready, drain and stir into the cheese sauce. Serve, or purée to the desired consistency.
- Chop the cauliflower roughly, then stir into the macaroni cheese just before serving.

White fishcakes

 Makes 8 small fishcakes and takes 30 minutes.

Fish is one of the most mineral-rich foods you can consume and is packed with omega 3 and vitamin D. These are essential as they are both conducive to healthy bone and brain development.

300 g / 11 oz / 1 ½ cups potatoes, peeled and chopped

1 small carrot, peeled and chopped

115 g / 4 oz / ½ cup skinless, boneless haddock or cod fillet, steamed or poached and flaked

2 tsp chopped chives

1 tbsp butter, melted

flour, for dusting

sunflower oil, for frying

- Cook the potatoes and carrot in boiling water for about 10 minutes, until tender. Drain and leave to dry and cool slightly.
- Put the potatoes, carrots, fish, chives and melted butter into a bowl and mash together.
- Put some flour into a bowl and dust your hands. Shape the potato mixture into eight patties. Lightly dust each fishcake with flour, then chill until firm.
- Heat a little oil in a non-stick frying pan and cook the fishcakes for about 3 minutes each side until golden brown. Drain on kitchen paper, then serve.

Salmon and potato cakes

 Makes 8 small fishcakes and takes 30 minutes.

These savoury fishcakes are deliciously moreish and are just as good eaten cold the next day. Serve with a side of fresh garden peas, green beans or broccoli for a satisfying, wholesome meal.

300 g / 11 oz / 1 ½ cups potatoes, peeled and chopped

1 small carrot, peeled and chopped

1 small skinless, boneless salmon fillet, cooked and flaked

2 tsp chopped chives

1 tbsp butter, melted

flour, for dusting

sunflower oil, for frying

- Cook the potatoes and carrot in boiling water for about 10 minutes, until tender. Drain and leave to dry and cool slightly.
- Put the potatoes, carrots, salmon, chives and melted butter into a bowl and mash together.
- Put some flour into a bowl and dust your hands. Shape the potato mixture into eight patties. Lightly dust each fishcake with flour and then chill until firm.
- Heat a little oil in a non-stick frying pan and cook the fishcakes for about 3 minutes each side until golden brown. Drain on kitchen paper, then serve.

Pea and carrot savoury pancakes

Makes 8 portions and takes 20 minutes.

Savoury pancakes are ideal for a healthy lunchtime meal. They are delicious served warm, but if you have any leftovers they can be kept chilled in a sealed box and used as a snack the next day.

1 egg
200 ml / 7 fl. oz / ¾ cup milk
100 g / 3 ½ oz / ¾ cup self-raising flour
1 small carrot, grated
1 tbsp canned sweetcorn kernels
2 tbsp frozen petit pois, defrosted
2 tbsp Cheddar cheese, grated
sunflower oil, for frying

- Put the egg and milk into a bowl and beat with a fork. Add the flour and beat until smooth, then stir in the carrot, sweetcorn, peas and cheese.
- Heat a little oil in a non-stick frying pan and drop in tablespoons of the batter. Cook the pancakes for about 2 minutes each side until golden brown. Drain on kitchen paper, then serve.

Spinach and ricotta savoury pancakes

Makes 8 portions and takes 20 minutes.

These traditional flavours work well in pancake form! Why not try other combinations, too, such as chopped mushrooms and tomatoes or mixed vegetables and herbs?

1 egg
200 ml / 7 fl. oz / ¾ cup milk
100 g / 3 ½ oz / ¾ cup self-raising flour
2 tbsp ricotta cheese
3–4 tbsp spinach, chopped
sunflower oil for frying

- Put the egg and milk into a bowl and beat with a fork. Add the flour and beat until smooth, then stir in the ricotta and spinach.
- Heat a little oil in a non-stick frying pan and drop in tablespoons of the batter. Cook the pancakes for about 2 minutes each side until golden brown. Drain on kitchen paper, then serve.

Chicken with vegetables and noodles

 Makes 2 portions and takes 20 minutes.

To make this recipe vegetarian-friendly, omit the chicken and replace it with lightly fried tofu. This simple dish tastes great with a little fresh coriander for garnish, added before serving.

40 g / 1 ½ oz fine egg noodles

¼ red pepper, deseeded and cut into small fine strips

2 mangetout, finely sliced on the diagonal

1 spring onion (scallion), finely sliced

1 large courgette (zucchini), cut into long thin strips

2 tsp sunflower oil

½ small skinless, boneless chicken breast, cut into thin strips

5 tbsp coconut milk

- Put the noodles, pepper, mangetout, spring onion and courgette into a pan of boiling water. Cook for 3–5 minutes until the noodles are cooked and the vegetables are tender.

- Heat the oil in a small non-stick frying pan. Stir-fry the chicken for 5 minutes until cooked through. Drain the noodles and vegetables, reserving some cooking liquid. Add the noodles and vegetables to the chicken in the pan.

- Stir in the coconut milk and a little of the cooking liquid to thin to the desired consistency. Either serve as it is or mash to a coarse purée.

Creamy chicken curry

Makes 2 portions and takes 25 minutes.

This flavoursome recipe uses mild spices, combined with the natural sweetness of fruit, for a warming meal. Gradually introduce your child to spices, starting with mild flavours such as cinnamon and nutmeg before trying anything hotter!

2 tsp sunflower oil

½ skinless, boneless chicken breast, finely diced

½ small onion, finely chopped

1 small carrot, cut in matchsticks

2 tsp mild korma curry paste

150 ml / 5 fl. oz / ⅔ cup low-sodium chicken stock

½ small dessert apple, peeled, cored and diced

2 ready-to-eat dried apricots, chopped

100 ml / 3 ½ fl. oz / ½ cup coconut milk

1 tsp chopped fresh coriander (cilantro)

- Heat the oil in a small non-stick frying pan and cook the chicken for 3–4 minutes until cooked. Remove and put to one side.

- Add the onion and carrot to the pan and cook for 1 minute. Stir in the korma paste and the chicken stock. Cook for 3–4 minutes.

- Add the apple, apricots, coconut milk and chicken to the pan. Cook gently for 5 minutes. Sprinkle with the coriander and serve with cooked rice.

Red pepper and goats' cheese sandwiches

Makes 1 sandwich and takes 5 minutes.

2 slices white or wholemeal bread, crusts removed

1 tbsp soft goats' cheese

1 tbsp red pepper, finely chopped

- Spread one slice of bread with the goats' cheese, then scatter over the chopped pepper.
- Top with the other slice of bread and cut the sandwich into small squares or fingers.

Avocado and egg sandwiches

Makes 1 sandwich and takes 5 minutes.

2 slices white or wholemeal bread, crusts removed

½ small avocado, mashed with 2 tsp lemon juice

½ hard-boiled egg, shelled and mashed

2 tsp mayonnaise

- Spread the mashed avocado over one slice of bread. Mix the egg with the mayonnaise and spread over the avocado.
- Top with the other slice of bread and cut the sandwich into small squares or fingers and serve alongside small cubes of hard cheese and wedges of hard-boiled egg.

Cucumber and hummus sandwiches

Makes 1 sandwich and takes 5 minutes.

2 slices white or wholemeal bread, crusts removed

1 tbsp hummus

1 tbsp cucumber, finely chopped

- Spread one slice of bread with the hummus, then scatter over the chopped cucumber.
- Top with the other slice of bread and cut the sandwich into small squares or fingers.

Sausage and vegetable pasta

Makes 3 portions and takes 20 minutes.

150 g / 5 oz / 1 cup macaroni, or small pasta shapes

2 tsp sunflower oil

½ medium onion, chopped

2 good quality chipolata sausages, cooked and thinly sliced

6 cherry tomatoes, halved

200 ml / 7 fl. oz / ¾ cup passata

3 tbsp Cheddar cheese, grated

- Cook the pasta according to packet instructions. Heat the oil in a small pan and add the onion, cooking for 5 minutes until soft. Add the sausage slices and tomatoes and cook for 3–4 minutes. Stir in the passata and cooked pasta. Heat for 1–2 minutes.
- Spoon the mixture into small heatproof dishes. Sprinkle over the cheese and place under a hot grill for a couple of minutes to brown.

NOTE: Not suitable for babies under 12 months.

Pasta with tomato and basil sauce

Makes 3 portions and takes 20 minutes.

150 g / 5 oz / 1 cup macaroni, or small pasta shapes

2 tsp olive oil

½ medium onion, chopped

1 carrot, peeled and diced

½ tsp dried oregano

200 g can chopped tomatoes

1 tbsp tomato purée

2 tsp fresh chopped basil

- Cook the pasta according to packet instructions. Heat the oil in a small pan and add the onion, carrot and dried oregano. Cook for 3–4 minutes. Add the chopped tomatoes, 3 tbsp water and tomato purée. Cook for 1–2 minutes.
- Stir in the pasta and the fresh basil.

NOTE: Not suitable for babies under 12 months.

Pasta with tomato and olive sauce

Makes 3 portions and takes 20 minutes.

150 g / 5 oz / 1 cup macaroni, or small pasta shapes

2 tsp olive oil

½ medium onion, chopped

1 carrot, peeled and diced

½ tsp dried oregano

200 g can chopped tomatoes

1 tbsp tomato purée

2 tsp fresh basil, chopped

6 black olives, chopped and pitted

- Cook the pasta according to pack instructions. Heat the oil in a small pan and add the onion, carrot and dried oregano. Cook for 3–4 minutes. Add the chopped tomatoes, 3 tbsp water and tomato purée. Cook for 1–2 minutes.
- Stir in the pasta, fresh basil and olives.

NOTE: Not suitable for babies under 12 months.

Baby huevos rancheros

 Makes 2 portions and takes 20 minutes.

2 tsp sunflower oil

2 eggs

2 corn tortillas

4 tbsp canned refried beans

60 g / 2 oz / ½ cup grated Cheddar cheese

To serve:

tomato salsa

sour cream

- Heat the oil in a small frying pan and fry the eggs. Cook for 2–3 minutes each side or until the yolks are cooked to the desired degree.
- Heat the tortillas in a hot frying pan for about 1 minute on each side. Put the tortillas on a plate, then spread with the refried beans. Sprinkle over the cheese and top with the fried eggs.
- Serve with tomato salsa and sour cream.

Chicken fajitas

Makes 8 mini fajitas and takes 25 minutes.

1 tbsp sunflower oil

1 small skinless, boneless chicken breast

½ red pepper, deseeded and cut into strips

½ yellow pepper, deseeded and cut into strips

1 small red onion, chopped

2 soft tortilla wraps

- Heat half the oil in a small non-stick frying pan and cook the chicken for 8–10 minutes, turning occasionally. Make sure the chicken is thoroughly cooked. Remove from the pan and cool, then cut into strips.
- Heat the remaining oil in the pan and cook the vegetables for 4–5 minutes until tender. Remove and cool.
- Heat a large frying pan and heat the tortillas, one at a time for a few seconds, until soft and pliable.
- Mix the chicken and vegetables together and divide between the tortilla wraps. Roll up and cut each tortilla into four.

Top tip

Little wraps make great finger foods for little ones at this vital stage of their development, and it's important for development to allow them to pick up their own food.

Don't be afraid to add mild herbs and spices to these dishes, as part of baby's exploration of new flavours. A little smoked paprika and cumin work wonders in a chicken fajita mix. Baby food doesn't need to be bland, and it's fine to introduce sophisticated flavours now.

Turkey burgers

 Makes 4 mini burgers and takes 15 minutes.

25 g / 1 oz / ½ cup fresh breadcrumbs
250 g / 9 oz / 1 cup minced turkey
1 tbsp carrot, finely grated
1 tbsp sweetcorn kernels, chopped
1 tsp fresh parsley, chopped
½ tsp Italian herb seasoning
1 tbsp sunflower oil

- Put all the ingredients, except for the oil, into a bowl and mix well together.
- Shape into four small patties. Heat the oil in a non-stick frying pan and cook the burgers for 3–4 minutes on each side until golden brown and cooked through.

Beef burgers

 Makes 4 mini burgers and takes 15 minutes.

25 g / 1 oz / ½ cup fresh breadcrumbs
250 g / 9 oz / 1 cup lean minced beef
1 tbsp carrot, finely grated
1 tbsp sweetcorn kernels, chopped
1 tsp fresh parsley, chopped
½ tsp Italian herb seasoning
1 tbsp sunflower oil

- Put all the ingredients, except for the oil, into a bowl and mix well together.
- Shape into four small patties. Heat the oil in a non-stick frying pan and cook the burgers for 3–4 minutes on each side until golden brown and cooked through.

Veggie burgers

 Makes 4 mini burgers and takes 15 minutes plus chilling.

1 medium sweet potato
1 tbsp carrot, grated
1 tbsp sweetcorn, chopped
1 tbsp petit pois
1 spring onion (scallion), finely chopped
3 tbsp Cheddar cheese, grated
1 egg
50 g / 2 oz / 1 cup fresh breadcrumbs
1 tbsp sunflower oil

- Peel, chop and boil the sweet potato. Drain well, mash and mix with the carrot, sweetcorn, petit pois, spring onion and cheese.
- Shape into four small patties and chill until firm.
- Beat the egg and spread the breadcrumbs on a plate. Dip the burgers in the egg and then coat in the breadcrumbs.
- Fry in the oil for 2–3 minutes each side until golden brown.

Pasta primavera

Makes 2 portions and takes 15 minutes.

This classic pasta dish is creamy, satisfying and a great option if you are busy and haven't got much time. Serve alongside steamed, iron-rich broccoli or other healthy greens for a balanced meal.

4 tbsp orzo

2 tbsp frozen peas

1 tbsp carrot, finely chopped

1 tomato, skinned, deseeded and chopped

1 tbsp crème fraiche

2 tsp Parmesan cheese, freshly grated

• Cook the orzo according to pack instructions, adding the peas and carrots halfway through the cooking time.

• Drain well and return the orzo and vegetables to the pan. Add the tomato and crème fraiche and stir over a medium heat for 1 minute. Serve sprinkled with the Parmesan.

Cheese and mushroom calzones

 Makes 2 calzones and takes 35 minutes.

Involving children in the kitchen is a great way to learn through play. Pizza-making is a good place to start, as little ones can get creative with toppings and experiment with different flavour combinations. Plus it makes great finger food!

1 tsp olive oil

knob of butter

150 g / 5 oz / 1 cup chestnut mushrooms, roughly chopped

220 g / 8 oz pack pizza base mix

50 g / 1 ¾ oz / ½ cup Gruyère cheese, grated

50 g / 1 ¾ oz / ½ cup mozzarella cheese, chopped

• Heat the oil and butter in a small pan and add the mushrooms. Cook for about 5 minutes until tender. Leave to cool.

• Heat the oven to 220°C (200°C fan) / 425F / gas 7. Make up the pizza base mix according to packet instructions.

• Divide the dough in half and roll each one out to a circle about 15 cm (6 in) in diameter. Put a little mushroom mix in the centre of each one and top with the cheeses.

• Dampen the edge of the dough, fold in half and press together to seal. Place on a baking tray and bake for about 15 minutes until risen and golden brown. Cool before serving.

Spinach and ricotta cannelloni

 Makes 3 portions and takes 40 minutes.

This is a great dinner to serve up to the whole family, or to freeze for another occasion. To save time, you could buy dried canneloni tubes rather than making your own.

250 ml / 9 fl. oz / 1 cup passata

200 g / 7 oz / 1 cup canned chopped tomatoes

300 g / 11 oz / 1 ½ cups ricotta cheese

125 g / 4 ½ oz / ½ cup frozen spinach, thawed and chopped

1 tbsp fresh basil, finely chopped

25 g / 1 oz / ¼ cup grated Parmesan cheese

3 fresh lasagne sheets

50 g / 1 ¾ oz mozzarella cheese, sliced

- Heat the oven to 190°C (170°C fan) / 375F / gas 5. Mix the passata and chopped tomatoes together, then spread half the tomato mixture over the base of a small, ovenproof dish.

- Put the ricotta, spinach, basil and Parmesan into a bowl and mix well together. Cut the lasagne sheets in half width-ways. Place a little of the ricotta mixture along the long side of each pasta piece and roll up to form a tube.

- Lay the cannelloni side by side in the dish. Spoon over the remaining tomato mixture.

- Top with the mozzarella slices and bake in the oven for 25 minutes until golden brown.

Roast vegetable lasagne

Makes 4 portions and takes 1 hour 15 minutes.

This healthy lasagne is packed with nutritious vegetables and plenty of flavour. Why not make double the mixture and freeze a lasagne for next week?

2 red peppers, deseeded and quartered

2 courgettes (zucchinis), thickly sliced

½ small aubergine (eggplant), cubed

1 red onion, peeled and cut into 6 wedges

4 plum tomatoes, quartered

2 tbsp olive oil

400 g / 14 oz / 2 cups canned chopped tomatoes

250 ml / 9 fl. oz / 1 cup passata

2 tbsp fresh basil, shredded

4–5 fresh, lasagne sheets

2 tbsp butter

2 tbsp flour

300 ml / 11 fl. oz / 1 cup full-fat milk

125 g / 4 ½ oz / 1 cup Cheddar cheese, grated

2 tbsp grated Parmesan

- Heat the oven to 220°C (200°C fan) / 425F / gas 7. Put the peppers, courgettes, aubergine, onion and tomatoes into a roasting tin. Drizzle over the oil, then bake in the oven for about 20 minutes until the vegetables are tender. Turn them over once or twice during cooking. Remove and cool and then cut into smaller pieces if necessary.

- Mix together the canned tomatoes, passata and basil. Spoon a little of this mixture into the base of a shallow oven proof dish. Mix the rest into the roasted vegetables.

- Place a layer of pasta over the base of the dish. Top with some of the vegetable mixture. Continue layering in this way ending with a layer of pasta.

- Melt the butter in a small pan. Stir in the flour and cook for a minute. Remove from the heat and gradually add the milk, stirring continuously. Bring to the boil and cook for a minute. Add the Cheddar cheese and stir well.

- Pour the cheese sauce over the lasagne, then sprinkle over the grated Parmesan. Reduce the oven heat to 180°C / 160°C fan / 350F / gas 4. Bake the lasagne for 30–40 minutes until golden brown. Leave to stand for 5 minutes before serving.

Chicken and vegetable couscous

❄ *Makes 2 portions and takes 15 minutes.*

Couscous is a very versatile ingredient and works really well with this chicken and veg combo.
It's easy, tasty and can even be eaten cool the next day, so you don't have to throw out those leftovers.

½ skinless, boneless chicken breast
fillet chopped

250 ml / 9 fl. oz / 1 cup water,
or low-sodium chicken stock

4 tbsp frozen mixed vegetables, such
as peas and carrots

50 g / 1 ¾ oz / ⅓ cup couscous

25 g / 1 oz / ⅛ cup butter, melted

- Put the chicken in a small pan with the water or stock. Bring to
the boil and simmer gently for about 8 minutes until the chicken
is tender. Add the frozen vegetables and cook for 3 minutes.
Drain the chicken and vegetables, reserving the cooking liquid.

- Measure out 100 ml / 3 ½ fl. oz / ½ cup of the cooking liquid and
bring to the boil. Put the couscous into a bowl and pour over the
cooking liquid. Cover with cling film and leave for 5 minutes until
swollen and fluffy.

- Mix together the couscous, chicken and vegetables. Stir in the
melted butter and serve.

Kedgeree

Makes 2 portions and takes 50 minutes.

This dish is packed with nutrients and bursting with wonderful flavours. Fish is a great way to
incorporate amino acids and protein into your baby's diet, so it's worth introducing this early – even
if you're not a fish fan yourself!

200 g / 7 oz skinless cod fillet

150 ml / 5 fl. oz / ⅔ cup full-fat milk

2 tbsp butter

½ onion, finely chopped

1 tsp mild curry powder

150 g / 5 oz / ¾ cup long grain rice

500 ml / 18 fl. oz / 2 cups low-sodium
vegetable stock

2–3 tbsp defrosted frozen peas

2–3 tbsp drained, canned sweetcorn
kernels

2 eggs, hard boiled, shelled and
chopped

1 tbsp flat leaf parsley, finely chopped

- Put the cod into a small, deep pan and pour in the milk.
Bring to the boil, then reduce heat to low, cover and simmer
for about 3–5 minutes or until cooked.

- Remove the fish with a draining spoon, reserving the milk.
Flake with a fork, taking care to remove any bones.

- Melt the butter in a frying pan and cook the onion for 2–3 minutes.
Add the curry powder and cook for 1 minute, then add the rice and
stir well.

- Pour in the stock and the strained, reserved milk. Bring to the boil,
then reduce the heat, cover and simmer gently for about 15 minutes
until the rice is cooked and the liquid absorbed.

- Add the cod, peas, sweetcorn, eggs and parsley and fold in gently.
Heat for 1 minute, then serve.

Toad in the hole

Makes 4 portions and takes 35 minutes.

Kids love bite-sized foods, so these mini versions of a toad in the hole are bound to be popular! The Yorkshire pudding is easy for them to chew, and little cocktail sausages add a fun element.

2–3 tbsp sunflower oil

100 ml / 3 ½ fl. oz / ½ cup full-fat milk

2 eggs

7 tbsp plain (all-purpose) flour

12 mini cocktail sausages

- Heat the oven to 220°C (200°C fan) / 425F / gas 7. Put a little oil into the bottom of each section of a four-hole Yorkshire pudding tin.
- Put the milk, egg and flour into a small bowl and whisk to a smooth batter.
- Put the Yorkshire pudding tin in the oven for a few minutes until the oil is very hot.
- Divide the batter between the four sections, then add three sausages to the centre of each one. Bake for 20–25 minutes until well risen, golden brown and crisp.

Cottage pie

Makes 2 portions and takes 1 hour.

Cottage pie has always been a traditional family favourite. Its soft texture will go down a treat with your little one, while introducing him to new, more sophisticated flavours.

2 tsp vegetable oil

1 small onion, finely chopped

1 small carrot, finely chopped

200 g / 7 oz lean minced beef

1 tbsp plain (all-purpose) flour

250 ml / 9 fl. oz / 1 cup low-sodium beef stock

200 g / 7 oz / 1 cup canned chopped tomatoes

1 tsp Worcestershire sauce

500 g / 18 oz / 2 ½ cups potatoes, peeled and chopped

250 g / 9 oz / 1 ¼ cups sweet potato, peeled and chopped

1–2 tbsp milk

1 tbsp butter

- Heat the oil in a small pan and cook the onion and carrot for about 5 minutes until soft. Add the minced beef and cook for 2–3 minutes.
- Stir in the flour, then add the stock. Bring to the boil, stirring. Add the tomatoes and the Worcestershire sauce. Cover and simmer for 15 minutes.
- While the mince is cooking, put the potatoes and sweet potato in a pan of water. Bring to the boil and cook for 10–15 until tender. Drain and mash with the butter and enough milk to mix to a creamy consistency.
- Heat the oven to 190°C (170°C fan) / 375F / gas 5.
- Spoon the mince into two individual ovenproof dishes. Top with the mashed potato. Bake in the oven for 10–15 minutes until golden brown.

Fruity Moroccan chicken

✱ *Makes 2 portions and takes 35 minutes.*

This fragrant and fruity dish is suitable for your whole family, not just your baby. With recipes like this in your repertoire, you'll be able to accommodate everyone with one meal, making your life a lot easier!

2 tbsp olive oil

1–2 tsp ras-el-hanout spice

1 skinless, boneless chicken breast fillet

1 small onion, finely chopped

200 g / 7 oz / 1 cup canned chopped tomatoes

100 ml / 3 ½ fl. oz / ½ cup water

4 ready-to-eat dried apricots, chopped

2 tbsp sultanas, roughly chopped

a pinch ground cinnamon

couscous, to serve

- Mix 1 tbsp of the olive oil with the spice mix. Rub the mix all over the chicken breast.
- Cut the chicken into thick slices. Heat the remaining oil in a pan, then add the chicken pieces and onion and cook for 5 minutes.
- Add the tomatoes, water, apricots, sultanas and cinnamon. Cover and simmer for 20 minutes until the chicken is tender.
- Cut the chicken into smaller pieces if necessary, then serve with couscous.

Courgette and salmon couscous

Makes 2 portions and takes 25 minutes.

Fish contains amino acids, making it a fantastic source of protein. Paired with couscous, cucumber and avocado, this salmon salad is a healthy, wholesome dish that contains a whole host of nutrients!

1 skinless, boneless salmon fillet

8 tbsp couscous or bulgar wheat

125 ml / 4 ½ fl. oz / ½ cup low-sodium vegetable stock

6 cm (2 ½ in) cucumber, finely diced

½ ripe avocado, peeled and chopped

1 tbsp natural yogurt

1 tbsp light olive oil

2 tsp lemon juice

- Steam or poach the salmon fillet for 5–8 minutes until cooked. Allow to cool, then flake the fish with a fork carefully, checking for any bones.
- Put the couscous into a bowl. Heat the stock to just boiling, then pour it over the couscous. Cover and leave for 10 minutes.
- Fluff up the couscous with a fork. Add the salmon flakes, cucumber and avocado.
- Mix together the yogurt, oil and lemon juice and pour over the salad. Gently mix everything together and serve.

Bread and butter pudding

Makes 4 portions and takes 1 hour and 20 minutes, including soaking time.

Children can enjoy this decadent dessert with a glass of milk as a yummy bedtime treat! This is a great dish to share with the whole family.

25 g / 1 oz / ⅛ cup butter, plus extra for greasing

6 slices day-old bread

50 g / 1 ¾ oz / ⅓ cup sultanas

1 tsp ground cinnamon

400 ml / 14 fl. oz / 1 ⅔ cups full-fat milk

2 eggs

2 tbsp caster (superfine) sugar

- Grease a 1 litre (2 pint) shallow, ovenproof dish. Cut the crusts off the bread. Spread each slice with butter, then cut into triangles.
- Arrange a layer of bread, butter side up, in the bottom of the dish. Sprinkle over the sultanas and cinnamon, then top with the remaining bread.
- Heat the milk gently until very hot but not boiling. Put the eggs and three quarters of the sugar in a bowl and whisk together.
- Add the milk to the eggs mixing well and then pour the mixture evenly over the bread. Leave to stand for 30 minutes.
- Heat the oven to 180°C (160°C fan) / 350F / gas 4.
- Sprinkle with the remaining sugar and bake for 30–40 minutes until the custard is set and the top is golden brown.

Choc chip muffins

Makes 12 muffins and takes 40 minutes.

These delightful mini treats are perfect for picnics, travel and lunch boxes to keep little ones happy. The chocolate chips can be replaced with unsweetened dried cranberries or sultanas for a healthier snack.

125 g / 4 ½ oz / ½ cup butter, softened

125 g / 4 ½ oz / ½ cup caster (superfine) sugar

2 eggs, beaten

125 g / 4 ½ oz / 1 cup self-raising flour

1 tsp vanilla extract

100 g / 3 ½ oz / ½ cup chocolate chips

- Heat the oven to 180°C (160°C fan) / 350F / gas 4. Put 12 small paper cases in a 12-hole bun tin.
- Put the butter and sugar into a bowl, then beat together until pale and fluffy. Add the beaten eggs a little at a time, gradually adding some of the flour.
- Incorporate the remaining flour, vanilla extract and chocolate chips.
- Spoon the mixture into the prepared cases and bake in the oven for 10–15 minutes until well risen and golden brown.

Apple crumble and yogurt

 Makes 6 portions and takes 50 minutes.

Apple crumble has always been a classic dessert, and there's no reason that your baby can't enjoy this fruity favourite as well! This simple version is ideal for the whole family and well worth the effort. Serve with warmed custard as an alternative.

500 g / 18 oz cooking **apples, peeled and cored**

2 tbsp water

2 tbsp caster (superfine) **sugar**

For the crumble:

180 g / 6 oz / 1 ¼ cups **self-raising flour**

80 g / 3 oz / ⅓ cup **butter**

125 g / 4 ½ oz / ¾ cups **soft brown sugar**

Greek yogurt, to serve

- Heat the oven to 190°C (170°C fan) / 375F / gas 5.
- Chop the apples into small pieces and mix with the sugar. Place into a small ovenproof pie dish. Sprinkle over the water.
- Put the flour into a bowl and rub in the butter, then mix in the brown sugar. Spoon the crumble evenly over the fruit and cook for about 30 minutes until the fruit is soft and the crumble golden.
- Serve with Greek yogurt.

Peach and raspberry crumble with yogurt

Makes 6 portions and takes 50 minutes.

This fruity crumble is bursting with refreshing, sweet flavours! As well as making an irresistible dessert, there's plenty of health-boosting fruits in there that your little one will love. The perfect treat for special occasions.

5–6 firm but ripe **peaches, peeled, stoned and chopped**

2 handfuls fresh **raspberries**

1 tbsp water

For the crumble:

180 g / 6 oz / 1 ¼ cups **self-raising flour**

80 g / 3 oz / ⅓ cup **butter**

125 g / 4 ½ oz / ¾ cups **soft brown sugar**

Greek yogurt, to serve

- Heat the oven to 190°C (170°C fan) / 375F / gas 5.
- Place the chopped peaches and raspberries into a small ovenproof pie dish. Sprinkle over the water.
- Put the flour into a bowl and rub in the butter, then mix in the brown sugar. Spoon the crumble evenly over the fruit and cook for about 30 minutes until the fruit is soft and the crumble golden.
- Serve with Greek yogurt.

Chocolate bananas

Makes 6 portions and takes 30 minutes.

Rather than giving your little one a chunk of chocolate, spend a little extra time making these delicious chocolate bananas for a half-healthy treat! Babies will love this flavour combination, and you'll be satisfied that she's getting some nutritional benefits, too.

250 g / 9 oz / 1 ½ cups plain dark
    chocolate, chopped

2 bananas, peeled

6 wooden lolly (popsicle) sticks

hundreds and thousands

- Melt the chocolate in a bowl over a pan of simmering water. Once melted, remove from the heat and allow to cool slightly until of coating consistency.
- Line a baking tray with greaseproof paper.
- Cut each banana into three and insert a wooden lolly stick in one end of each one. Dip the bananas into the melted chocolate, then turn until well coated in chocolate. Sprinkle with hundreds and thousands and place on the prepared tray.
- Place in the fridge until firm.

Chocolate pudding

Makes 4 portions and takes 20 minutes.

These super-easy, quick puds are a great treat for after dinner. Why not add some raspberries to the cake mix for a fruity burst? These small portions are the perfect size for little fingers, and will make sure your baby isn't having too many naughty treats!

80 g / 3 oz / ⅓ cup butter, plus extra
    for greasing

125 g / 4 ½ oz / ¾ cup plain dark
    chocolate, chopped

2 egg yolks

2 tbsp caster (superfine) sugar

3 egg whites

- Heat the oven to 180°C (160°C fan) / 350F / gas 4. Lightly grease four 6 cm (3 in) ramekin dishes.
- Melt the butter and chocolate together in a small bowl over a pan of simmering water.
- In another bowl mix together the egg yolks and sugar. Stir in the melted and cooled chocolate.
- Whisk the egg whites to soft peaks and fold into the chocolate mixture. Spoon into the prepared dishes and bake in the oven for 5–8 minutes.

Strawberry and orange jelly boats

Makes 16 boats and takes 2 hours 25 minutes, including time to set.

Kids love the wibbly wobbly nature of jelly, so these little boats are great for parties. Fun shapes engage young children and will also help them to learn, understand and develop.

4 oranges, halved

135 g / 5 oz pack strawberry jelly

135 g / 5 oz pack orange jelly

For decoration:

16 cocktail sticks

4 sheets rice paper, cut into triangles

- Carefully remove the inside flesh of the oranges. Scrape out the membrane, taking care not to make a hole in the skin of the oranges.
- Make up the jellies according to the pack instructions but only use half the water suggested for each. Pour the jellies into the orange halves, filling to the top. Chill until set.
- Trim the orange halves so the skin is level with the jelly. Cut each orange in half. Push a cocktail stick into each rice paper triangle to make sails. Push a sail into each orange jelly boat.

Top tip

Jelly is so simple, and yet so effective! It comes in a variety of flavours, so why not collect some fun moulds to make great jelly shapes?

Toddlers will want to get involved in the gooey jelly-making process, so be careful when handling hot water around them. Letting them pick out moulds and make embellishments, like these sails, are a great way for them to join in the fun.

Banana bread

 Makes 1 loaf and takes 1 hour and 20 minutes.

For a delicious variation to this classic recipe, try adding some raisins, chocolate chips or chopped walnuts to the cake mixture before baking.

300 g / 11 oz / 2 cups plain (all-purpose) flour

1 tsp bicarbonate of (baking) soda

125 g / 4 ½ oz / ½ cup butter

200 g / 7 oz / 1 cup soft brown sugar

2 eggs, beaten

4 over ripe bananas, peeled and mashed

90 ml / 3 fl. oz / ⅔ cup buttermilk or natural yogurt

1 tsp vanilla extract

- Heat the oven to 180°C (160°C fan) / 350F / gas 4. Grease and line a 20 cm x 12.5 cm (8 in x 5 in) loaf tin.

- Sieve together the flour and bicarbonate of soda. Put the butter and sugar into a bowl and beat together until creamy. Add the eggs, mashed bananas, buttermilk and vanilla extract. Mix well, then fold in the flour. Spoon the mixture into the tin.

- Bake in the oven for 45–60 minutes until well risen and golden brown.

Tzatziki dip

Makes 6 portions and takes 10 minutes.

125 g / 4 ½ oz / ½ cup natural Greek
   yogurt

⅓ peeled cucumber, deseeded, grated
   and squeezed dry in a tea towel

2 tsp lemon juice

- Place the ingredients into a small bowl and mix together.
- Serve accompanied with sticks of carrot, celery, cucumber and pepper, apple slices and strips of pitta bread.

Satay dip

Makes 6 portions and takes 10 minutes.

130 g / 4 ½ oz / ½ cup smooth peanut
   butter

80 ml / 3 fl. oz / ⅓ cup light coconut
   milk

1 tsp low-sodium soy sauce

2 tsp sweet chilli sauce

- Place the ingredients into a small bowl and mix together.
- Serve accompanied with sticks of carrot, celery, cucumber and pepper, apple slices and strips of pitta bread.

NOTE: Not suitable for children under 12 months, or those with a familial history of peanut allergy.

Cream cheese dip

Makes 6 portions and takes 10 minutes.

125 g / 4 ½ oz / ½ cup light cream
   cheese

2 tbsp natural Greek yogurt

- Place the ingredients into a small bowl and mix together.
- Serve accompanied with sticks of carrot, celery, cucumber and pepper, apple slices and strips of pitta bread.

Apple and cinnamon flapjacks

Makes 12 flapjacks and takes 1 hour and 15 minutes.

These flapjacks taste delicious with some chopped, dried apricots or raisins added to the mixture. They make great lunch-box fillers for eating on the move, and are a tasty snack for the whole family.

125 g / 4 ½ oz / ½ cup butter

80 g / 3 oz / ⅓ cup light brown sugar

3 tbsp golden syrup

250 g / 9 oz / 2 ½ cups rolled oats

1 tsp ground cinnamon

1 dessert apple, peeled, cored and grated

2 tbsp sunflower seeds

For the topping:

3 tbsp golden syrup

1 dessert apple, cored and thinly sliced

- Heat the oven to 180°C (160°C fan) / 350F / gas 4. Grease a 20 cm (8 in) shallow square cake tin.
- Melt the butter, sugar and syrup together in a large pan over a low heat. Remove from the heat and stir in the oats, cinnamon, apple and sunflower seeds. Mix well.
- Press evenly into the tin and bake for about 35–40 minutes until golden brown. Leave to cool for 10 minutes and then cut into 12 squares.
- To decorate, heat the golden syrup in a small non-stick frying pan. Add the apple slices and poach in the syrup, over a medium heat, for 3–4 minutes.
- Carefully place the slices on top of the flapjacks and leave to cool.

Chicken, spring onion and pear pittas

Makes 1 portion and takes 5 minutes.

1 small pitta bread, or small bap

1–2 slices cooked roast chicken, chopped

1 small spring onion (scallion), finely chopped

4 slices cucumber, quartered

2–3 basil leaves, chopped

¼ ripe pear, peeled, cored and sliced

2 tsp natural yogurt

- Cut the pitta in half and open out the pocket. If using a bap, cut in half width ways.
- Gently toss together the remaining ingredients and fill the pitta pockets, or place the filling on the base of the bap, top with the lid and cut in half to serve.

Lamb with mint yogurt pittas

Makes 1 portion and takes 5 minutes.

1 small pitta bread, or small bap

1 small slice of cooked roast lamb, chopped

1 small spring onion (scallion), finely chopped

4 slices cucumber, quartered

2–3 mint leaves, chopped

¼ dessert apple, peeled, cored and chopped

2 tsp natural yogurt

- Cut the pitta in half and open out the pocket. If using a bap, cut in half width ways.
- Gently toss together the remaining ingredients and fill the pitta pockets, or place the filling on the base of the bap, top with the lid and cut in half to serve.

Ham and pea frittatas

Makes 12 mini fritattas and takes 40 minutes.

Bite-sized dishes make great finger foods for babies and these tasty frittatas are perfect for this stage of weaning. They contain a variety of food groups, which will help give your baby the balanced diet that she needs.

2 tbsp sunflower oil

½ onion, finely chopped

8 eggs

50 ml / 1 ¾ fl. oz / ¼ cup milk

2 tbsp cornflour (cornstarch)

4 tbsp peas

150 g / 5 oz / ¾ cup cooked ham, thinly sliced

- Heat the oven to 190°C (170°C fan) / 375F / gas 5. Grease 12 non-stick muffin tins.
- Heat the oil in a small frying pan and cook the onion over a low heat for about 5 minutes until soft. Remove from the heat.
- Put the eggs, milk and cornflour into a bowl and whisk together. Stir in the peas and onion.
- Line the muffin tins with the ham, making sure the base and sides are covered. Spoon in the egg mixture and bake in the oven for about 20 minutes until set. Cool before removing from the tin.

Spinach and cheese frittatas

Makes 12 mini fritattas and takes 40 minutes.

Spinach is a highly nutritious green vegetable, so it's a great ingredient in these tasty little frittatas. Combined with cheese, these savoury bites make great party food or snacks.

2 tbsp sunflower oil

½ onion, finely chopped

8 eggs

50 ml / 1 ¾ fl. oz / ¼ cup milk

2 tbsp cornflour (cornstarch)

4 tbsp spinach, chopped

2 tbsp Parmesan cheese, grated

- Heat the oven to 190°C (170°C fan) / 375F / gas 5.
- Heat the oil in a small frying pan and cook the onion over a low heat for about 5 minutes until soft. Remove from the heat.
- Put the eggs, milk and cornflour into a bowl and whisk together. Stir in the spinach and Parmesan.
- Line the base of each section of a 12 hole muffin tin with a circle of greaseproof paper and grease well. Spoon in the egg mixture and bake in the oven for about 20 minutes until set. Cool before removing from the tin.

Mini arancini

Makes 12 rice balls and takes 40 minutes plus chilling time.

600 ml / 1 pint / 2 ½ cups low-sodium
  vegetable stock

150 g / 5 oz / ⅔ cup risotto rice

2 eggs

1 tbsp butter, melted

1 tbsp grated Parmesan cheese

100 g / 3 ½ oz / 1 cup mozzarella
  cheese, chopped

plain (all-purpose) flour for dusting

80 g / 3 oz / ¾ cup dried breadcrumbs

sunflower oil for frying

To serve:

tomato sauce, or salsa

- Put the stock into a small pan and bring to the boil. Add the rice and cook for 15–20 minutes until tender. Drain the rice and tip into a bowl and cool.
- Add 1 egg, beaten, the butter, Parmesan and mozzarella, then mix well. With damp hands, shape the mixture into small balls. Place a little flour on a plate and roll the balls in it.
- Beat the remaining egg and put into a shallow dish. Put the breadcrumbs into another shallow dish. Take one ball at a time and dip in the egg and then roll in the breadcrumbs to coat. Place the balls on a plate and chill for 30 minutes.
- Heat a little oil in a frying pan and cook the rice balls for about 5 minutes, turning frequently, until golden brown. Drain on kitchen paper. Serve with tomato sauce or salsa.

Mini arancini with tomato

Makes 12 rice balls and takes 40 minutes plus chilling time.

600 ml / 1 pint / 2 ½ cups low-sodium
  vegetable stock

150 g / 5 oz / ⅔ cup risotto rice

2 eggs

1 tbsp butter, melted

1 tbsp grated Parmesan cheese

100 g / 3 ½ oz / 1 cup mozzarella,
  chopped

6 sun-blush tomatoes, halved

plain (all-purpose) flour for dusting

80 g / 3 oz / ¾ cup dried breadcrumbs

sunflower oil for frying

To serve:

tomato sauce, or salsa

- Put the stock into a small pan and bring to the boil. Add the rice and cook for 15–20 minutes until tender. Drain the rice and tip into a bowl and cool.
- Add 1 egg, beaten, butter, Parmesan and mozzarella, then mix well. With damp hands, shape the mixture into small balls, then push half a sun-blush tomato into each ball. Place a little flour on a plate and roll the balls in it.
- Beat the remaining egg and put into a shallow dish. Put the breadcrumbs into another shallow dish. Take one ball at a time and dip in the egg and then roll in the breadcrumbs to coat. Place the balls on a plate and chill for 30 minutes.
- Heat a little oil in a frying pan and cook the rice balls for about 5 minutes, turning frequently, until golden brown. Drain on kitchen paper. Serve with tomato sauce or salsa.

Muesli bars

Makes 20 bars and takes 40 minutes.

100 g / 3 ½ oz / 1 cup self-raising flour

300 g / 11 oz / 3 ½ cups rolled oats

50 g / 1 ¾ oz / ½ cup desiccated coconut

50 g / 1 ¾ oz / ¼ cup sesame seeds

100 g / 3 ½ oz / ½ cup sunflower seeds

50 g / 1 ¾ oz / ¼ cup dried cranberries

50 g / 1 ¾ oz / ¼ cup dried dates, chopped

200 g / 7 oz / 1 cup dark soft brown sugar

200 g / 7 oz / 1 cup butter

125 g / 4 ½ oz / ⅓ cup golden (light corn) syrup

- Heat the oven to 180°C (160°C fan) / 350F / gas 4. Grease and line a 18 cm x 28 cm (7 in x 11 in) shallow cake tin.

- In a bowl mix together the flour, oats, coconut, sesame seeds, sunflower seeds, cranberries, dates and sugar.

- Put the butter and syrup into a small pan and stir together, over a medium heat, until melted. Pour into the oat mixture and mix together well.

- Spoon the mixture into the tin and press down well. Bake in the oven for about 25 minutes.

- Leave to cool and then cut into bars.

Top tip

Muesli bars are a great on-the-go snack. They will keep well in a sealed box and won't create too much mess when you're out and about.

You can mix and match other seeds and fruits into this versatile recipe for a bit of variety – chopped dried apricots or raisins would both work well.

Oat and honey biscuits

Makes 12 biscuits and takes 30 minutes

These tasty snacks will keep for a few days in an airtight box and you can easily double up the quantities to make a larger batch.

125 g / 4 ½ oz / ½ cup butter

2 tbsp clear honey

1 tsp bicarbonate of (baking) soda

125 g / 4 ½ oz / ½ cup caster (superfine) sugar

125 g / 4 ½ oz / 1 ¼ cups plain (all-purpose) flour

180 g / 6 oz / 1 ¾ cups rolled oats

- Heat the oven to 180°C (160°C fan) / 350F / gas 4 and line 2 baking trays with greaseproof paper.
- Melt the butter and honey in a small pan over a low heat. Remove from the heat and stir in the bicarbonate of soda.
- Put the sugar, flour and oats into a mixing bowl. Add the honey mixture, stir and cool slightly.
- Drop spoonfuls of the mixture onto the prepared trays. Bake for 10–15 minutes until golden brown. Cool on the tray for 5 minutes and then place on a cooling rack.

NOTE: Not suitable for babies under 12 months.

Curried lentil cakes

 Makes 8 cakes and takes 25 minutes.

The gentle hint of spice in these healthy rice cakes is great for some added interest at snack time. If your baby isn't keen, you can reduce the quantity of korma paste to start with and build it up gradually.

sunflower oil, for frying

½ small onion, finely chopped

1 tsp mild korma paste

100 g / 3 ½ oz / ½ cup red lentils

250 ml / 9 fl. oz / 1 cup low-sodium vegetable stock

1 medium carrot, grated

1 tsp fresh coriander (cilantro), finely chopped

2 slices wholemeal bread, made into breadcrumbs

1 large egg, beaten

- Heat 2 tsp of the oil in small pan, then add the onion and cook for 1 minute. Stir in the korma paste and cook for a further minute.
- Add the lentils and stock. Simmer for about 10 minutes until the lentils are very soft. Add the carrot and coriander, then cook for a few more minutes until the mixture begins to dry. Remove the pan from the heat and cool.
- Stir in the breadcrumbs, then add the egg and shape into eight small patties.
- Heat a little oil in a non stick frying pan and cook the patties for 2–3 minutes on each side.

Following a healthy plan

If you are still feeling none the wiser by the time you have got to this stage of the book, don't worry. When I weaned I felt that a lot of information out there was either contradictory or confusing; no two camps were saying exactly the same thing. That's because no two babies are alike. The overriding message that comes through is the importance of what not to do. For example, no cows' milk, salt or honey before 12 months. Even if you want or feel the need to wean early, never start before 17 weeks. And finally if at first you don't succeed, try, try... try again. You may be tasked with convincing your baby to try a food 15 times before the little man decides he likes it!

The weaning experience can range from frustrating to fantastic on any given day. You can be filled with joy and reduced to tears in the space of a meal! Your white kitchen walls and whatever you are wearing become a splash back for everything baby throws back. Your nappy experience becomes an education in itself – how could someone so little produce so much and create such a stench. Who knew that sweetcorn comes out as it goes in! Your anxiety levels heighten and with every gag and guffaw you fear for the worst. Is this a choke or a simple cough?

As your baby grows you soon realize that it's not only your baby learning with every new phase in life, you too are a novice. You are enthusiastic about doing it right but on edge about doing it wrong. As a first-time mother I felt the various stages of looking after a baby were like taking up running. At the start you feel pretty useless and clueless, but in the space of a few days you have got it sussed. You run to the end of the street and in no time at all you proudly call yourself a runner. Weaning is a bit like this. You start off saying your baby

is 'being weaned' like some other force is doing it for you. Then you progress to proudly announcing 'I am weaning my baby'. It might seem like a tiny difference but that very statement for me was the definition of being in control. I was up and running and on the right track.

By the time I wrote this book my own baby was weaned. Part of me wishes I had actually made an effort to read a book on the subject before she made a transition to solids. But part of me knows that while I defiantly didn't do it by the book – because I didn't buy one – I didn't do too badly. While researching this book I've had moments of horror thinking about things that I did that I shouldn't have. I have had moments of clarity with things that seem so obvious now but that I was oblivious to back then. I've also had moments of hysterical laughter as I recall all the pulping, mashing, spluttering, splattering, pooing and farting it took before we eventually reached the holy grail of family food. Like every milestone in your child's life, the weaning stage is transient. In the middle of all the mess and mayhem, take a minute to enjoy the moment. This is a truly special time for all the family.

CUCUMBER
Chicken, spring onion and pear pittas, 115
Courgette and salmon couscous, 99
Cucumber and hummus sandwiches, 83
Lamb with mint yogurt pittas, 115
Tzatziki dip, 111

CURRY PASTE
Creamy chicken curry, 80
Curried lentil cakes, 123

CURRY POWDER
Kedgeree, 95

DATES
Muesli bars, 120

EGGS
Apple and raspberry custard, 54
Avocado and egg sandwiches, 83
Baby huevos rancheros, 87
Banana bread, 108
Bread and butter pudding, 100
Choc chip muffins, 100
Chocolate pudding, 104
Curried lentil cakes, 123
Eggy bread, 60
Ham and pea frittatas, 116
Kedgeree, 95
Mini arancini, 119
Mini arancini with tomato, 119
Mini blueberry muffins, 63
Mini broccoli muffins, 63
Omelette with bacon, 60
Pancakes with banana and syrup, 71
Pancakes with fruit, 71
Pea and carrot savoury pancakes, 79
Raisin buns, 68
Scrambled egg, 60
Spinach and cheese frittatas, 116
Spinach and ricotta savoury pancakes, 79
Toad in the hole, 96
Veggie burgers, 88

FIGS
Fig and nectarine purée, 54

FLOUR, PLAIN (ALL-PURPOSE)
Banana bread, 108
Cheesy broccoli purée, 45
Cottage pie, 96
Mini blueberry muffins, 63
Oat and honey biscuits, 123
Pancakes with banana and syrup, 71
Pancakes with fruit, 71
Raisin buns, 68
Roast vegetable lasagne, 92
Toad in the hole, 96

FLOUR, SELF-RAISING
Apple crumble and yogurt, 103
Mini broccoli muffins, 63
Choc chip muffins, 100
Muesli bars, 120
Pea and carrot savoury pancakes, 79
Peach and raspberry crumble
    with yogurt, 103
Spinach and ricotta savoury pancakes, 79

GOLDEN SYRUP
Apple and cinnamon flapjacks, 112
Muesli bars, 120

GRAPES
Pancakes with fruit, 71

HADDOCK
White fishcakes, 76

HAM
Ham and pea frittatas, 116

HONEY
Oat and honey biscuits, 123

HUMMUS
Cucumber and hummus sandwiches, 83

JELLY
Strawberry and orange jelly boats, 107

KALE
Kale purée, 38

KIWI
Kiwi and banana smoothie, 49

LAMB
Lamb with mint yogurt pittas, 115

LEMON
Courgette and salmon couscous, 99
Tzatziki dip, 111

LENTILS
Carrot and tomato with lentils, 46
Curried lentil cakes, 123
Lentil stew, 42

MANGETOUT
Chicken with vegetables and noodles, 80

MANGO
Mango purée, 33
Rice pudding with mango, 50
Tropical fruit yogurt, 64

MAPLE SYRUP
Pancakes with banana and syrup, 71

MAYONNAISE
Avocado and egg sandwiches, 83

MELON
Melon and peach purée, 54

MILK
Apple and raspberry custard, 54
Blueberry porridge, 67
Bread and butter pudding, 100
Cheesy broccoli, 45
Cheesy pasta, 75
Cheesy pasta with bacon, 75
Cheesy pasta with cauliflower, 75
Cottage pie, 96
Eggy bread, 60
Ham and pea frittatas, 116
Kedgeree, 95
Mini blueberry muffins, 63
Mini broccoli muffins, 63
Pancakes with banana and syrup, 71
Pancakes with fruit, 71
Pea and carrot savoury pancakes, 79
Prune porridge, 67
Raisin and apple porridge, 67
Raisin buns, 68
Rice pudding, 50
Rice pudding with mango, 50
Scrambled egg, 60
Semolina with blueberries, 53
Spinach and cheese frittatas, 116
Spinach and ricotta savoury pancakes, 79
Toad in the hole, 96

MUSHROOMS
Cheese and mushroom calzones, 91

NECTARINE
Fig and nectarine purée, 54
Nectarine purée, 30

NOODLES
Chicken with vegetables and noodles, 80

OATS
Apple and cinnamon flapjacks, 112
Blueberry porridge, 67
Muesli bars, 120
Oatmeal porridge, 34
Oat and honey biscuits, 123
Prune porridge, 67
Raisin and apple porridge, 67

OLIVES
Pasta with tomato and olive sauce, 84

ONION
Chicken fajitas, 87
Cottage pie, 96
Creamy chicken curry, 80
Curried lentil cakes, 123
Fruity Moroccan chicken, 99
Ham and pea frittatas, 116
Kedgeree, 95
Pasta with tomato and basil sauce, 84
Pasta with tomato and olive sauce, 84
Roast vegetable lasagne, 92
Sausage and vegetable pasta, 84
Spinach and cheese frittatas, 116
Squash and spinach risotto, 42

ORANGE
Strawberry and orange jelly boats, 107

PAPAYA
Papaya and raspberry smoothie, 49
Tropical fruit yogurt, 64

PARSNIP
Parsnip purée, 27
Turkey and parsnip purée, 45

PASTA
Cheesy pasta, 75
Cheesy pasta with bacon, 75
Cheesy pasta with cauliflower, 75
Pasta primavera, 91
Pasta with tomato and basil sauce, 84
Pasta with tomato and olive sauce, 84
Roast vegetable lasagne, 92
Sausage and vegetable pasta, 84
Spinach and ricotta cannelloni, 92

PEACHES
Melon and peach purée, 54
Peach and raspberry crumble with
    yogurt, 103

PEANUT BUTTER
Satay dip, 111

PEAR
Chicken, spring onion and pear pittas, 115
Pear and apricot purée, 57

PEAS
Chicken and vegetable couscous, 95
Ham and pea frittatas, 116
Kedgeree, 95
Pasta primavera, 91
Pea and carrot savoury pancakes, 79
Pea and mint risotto, 72
Pea purée, 28
Salmon with peas and tomato, 46
Spinach and cheese frittatas, 116
Veggie burgers, 88

PEPPERS
Chicken fajitas, 87
Chicken with vegetables and noodles, 80

PICTURE CREDITS